P9-EDC-966

Weight Watchers Publishing Group

VP Content/Editor in Chief **Theresa DiMasi**

Creative Director **Ed Melnitsky**

Associate Editor **Katerina Gkionis**

Food Editor **Eileen Runyan**

Writer and Project Editor **Jackie Mills, MS, RD**

Contributing Editors **Lisa Chernick, Leslie Fink, MS, RD**

Photo Director **Marybeth Dulany**

Nutrition Consultants **Linda Wang, Ariella Sieger**

Production Manager **Alan Biederman**

Art Director **Daniela A. Hritcu**

Art/Production Assistant **Rebecca Kollmer**

Photographer **Romulo Yanes**

Food Stylist **Carrie Purcell**

Prop Stylist **Megan Hedgpeth**

SKU #11969

Printed in the USA

Front cover:
Pizza Margherita, page 142

Back cover:
Rigatoni with Roasted Squash, Kale and Pine Nuts, page 130

ABOUT WEIGHT WATCHERS INTERNATIONAL, INC.

Weight Watchers International, Inc. is the world's leading commercial provider of weight-management services, operating globally through a network of company-owned and franchise operations. Weight Watchers holds more than 36,000 meetings each week at which members receive group support and learn about healthy eating patterns, behavior modification, and physical activity. Weight Watchers provides innovative digital weight-management products through its websites, mobile sites, and apps. Weight Watchers is the leading provider of online subscription weight-management products in the world. In addition, Weight Watchers offers a wide range of products, publications, and programs for those interested in weight loss and weight control.

weightwatchers

dinners
in a flash

SIMPLE AND DELICIOUS MEALS UNDER 30 MINUTES

Huevos Mexicanos, 87

CONTENTS

ABOUT OUR RECIPES

While losing weight isn't only about what you eat, Weight Watchers realizes the critical role it plays in your success and overall good health. That's why our philosophy is to offer great-tasting, easy recipes that are nutritious as well as delicious. We create most of our recipes with the healthy and filling foods we love: lots of fresh fruits and vegetables, most of which have 0 SmartPoints® value, and satisfying lean proteins, which are low in SmartPoints. We also try to ensure that our recipes fall within the recommendations of the U.S. Dietary Guidelines for Americans so they support a diet that promotes health and reduces the risk for disease. If you have special dietary needs, consult with your health-care professional for advice on a diet that is best for you, then adapt these recipes to meet your specific nutritional needs.

get started, keep going, and enjoy good nutrition

At Weight Watchers, we believe that eating well makes life better, no matter where you are in your weight-loss journey. These delicious recipes are ideal, whether you're just getting started or have already reached your goals on the SmartPoints plan. Unlike other weight-loss programs, which focus solely on calories, the SmartPoints plan guides you toward healthier foods that are lower in sugar and saturated fat, and higher in protein. But this isn't a diet—all food is "in." Eating well should be fun, energizing, and delicious, so that healthy food choices become second nature. To get maximum satisfaction, we suggest you keep the following information in mind while preparing our recipes:

➡ SmartPoints values are given for each recipe. The SmartPoints for each ingredient is assigned based on the number of calories and the amount of saturated fat, sugar, and protein per the ingredient quantity. The SmartPoints for each ingredient are then added together and divided by the number of servings, and the result is rounded.

➡ Recipes include approximate nutritional information: They are analyzed for Calories (Cal), Total Fat, Saturated Fat (Sat Fat), Sodium (Sod), Total Carbohydrates (Total Carb), Sugar, Dietary Fiber (Fib), and Protein (Prot). The nutritional values are obtained from the Weight Watchers database, which is maintained by registered dietitians.

➡ To boost flavor, we often include fresh herbs or a squeeze of citrus instead of increasing the salt. If you don't have to restrict your sodium intake, feel free to add a touch more salt as desired.

➡ Recipes in this book that are designated gluten free do not contain any wheat (in all forms, including kamut, semolina, spelt, and triticale), barley, or rye, or any products that are made from these ingredients, such as breads, couscous, pastas, seitan, soy sauce, beer, malt vinegar, and malt beverages. Other foods such as salad dressings, Asian-style sauces, salsa and tomato sauce, shredded cheese, yogurt, and sour cream may be sources of gluten. Check ingredient labels carefully on packaged foods that we call for, as different brands of the same premade food product may or may not contain gluten. If you are following a gluten-free diet because you have celiac disease, please consult your health-care professional.

➡ Cook's Tip suggestions have a SmartPoints value of 0 unless otherwise stated.

➡ For information about the science behind lasting weight loss and more, please visit WeightWatchers.com/science.

calculations not what you expected?

SmartPoints for the recipes in this book are calculated without counting any fruits and most vegetables, but the nutrition information does include the nutrient content from fruits and vegetables. This means you may get a different SmartPoints value if you calculate the SmartPoints based on the nutrition. To allow for your "free" fruits and veggies, use the SmartPoints assigned to the recipes. Also, please note, when fruits and veggies are liquefied or pureed (as in a smoothie), their nutrient content is incorporated into the recipe calculations. These nutrients can increase the SmartPoints.

Alcohol is included in our SmartPoints calculations. Because alcohol information is generally not included on nutrition labels, it's not an option you can include when using the handheld or online calculator or the Weight Watchers app. But since we include the alcohol information that we get from our database in our recipes, you might notice discrepancies between the SmartPoints you see here in our recipes, and the values you get using the calculator. The SmartPoints listed for our recipes are the most accurate values.

simply filling (the no-count option)

If counting SmartPoints isn't your thing, try Simply Filling, a no-count technique. To follow it, eat just until satisfied, primarily from the list of Simply Filling foods found in your *Pocket Guide*. For more information see your member guidebook.

choosing ingredients

As you learn to eat healthier and add more wholesome foods to your meals, consider the following to help you choose foods wisely:

LEAN MEATS AND POULTRY

Purchase lean meats and poultry, and trim them of all visible fat before cooking. When poultry is cooked with the skin on, we recommend removing the skin before eating. Nutritional information for recipes that include meat, poultry, and fish is based on cooked, skinless boneless portions (unless otherwise stated), with the fat trimmed.

SEAFOOD

Whenever possible, our recipes call for seafood that is sustainable and deemed the most healthful for human consumption so that your choice of seafood is not only good for the oceans but also good for you. For more information about the best seafood choices and to download a pocket guide, go to the Environmental Defense Fund at seafood.edf.org or seafoodwatch.org.

PRODUCE

For best flavor, maximum nutrient content, and the lowest prices, buy fresh local produce such as vegetables, leafy greens, and fruits in season. Rinse them thoroughly before using, and keep a supply of cut-up vegetables and fruits in your refrigerator for convenient healthy snacks.

WHOLE GRAINS

Explore your market for whole-grain products such as whole wheat and whole-grain breads and pastas, brown rice, bulgur, barley, cornmeal, whole wheat couscous, oats, and quinoa to enjoy with your meals.

keep it fast & easy

4 TRICKS TO STREAMLINE DINNER

Finding time to cook fresh and healthy weeknight meals is a challenge for almost everyone. Busy schedules, late work hours, and kids' after-school commitments mean most of us rarely have time to prepare a meal and gather the family at the table for dinner.

We're here to help make weeknight meals fit into your hectic schedule. We walk you through **the foods you'll need to set up a basic pantry to cook healthy meals in a hurry, including refrigerated and frozen foods.** Then you'll find some **practical Sunday strategies** (they don't take long!) to ensure you and your family eat well all week, as well as **tips for organizing your kitchen** for efficient cooking.

The best part is that these 120 main-dish recipes take 30 minutes or less from start to finish. For even quicker meals, look for the Under 20 Minutes line for dishes that prep and cook in that time limit. And to round out your meals, **you'll find ideas for fuss-free salads, veggies, and sides on pages xiv–xv.**

1. STOCK UP

A well-stocked kitchen is not only inspiring but time-saving, too. When you keep basic ingredients on hand to prepare a variety of quick dishes, you're more likely to cook—and you can keep your grocery shopping to once a week.

When shopping for food, buy the best quality you can afford. Choose a good extra-virgin olive oil, well-made convenience foods, and fresh produce in season (buy local when possible and organic if your budget allows). Choose meats, poultry, dairy products, and eggs that come from humanely raised animals that are not given antibiotics or hormones. Your meals will only be as good as the ingredients you begin with.

Use these tips for stocking your pantry, refrigerator, and freezer with the basics you'll need to make weeknight cooking a pleasure.

stock the pantry

➥ Pantry items last a long time, so if your budget and storage space allow, create a stash of items that includes canned beans, broths, tomato products, coconut milk, tuna, salmon, and anchovies; dried pasta and noodles; rice and other grains; jarred olives, capers, and roasted red peppers packed in water; and oils and vinegars. Purchase them when they are on sale.

➥ Frequently used ingredients such as bread crumbs, flour, cornstarch, sugar, and dried herbs and spices are essential. If you enjoy Asian-inspired foods, keep a supply of soy sauce, hoisin sauce, chili-garlic sauce, and curry paste.

➥ Pantry produce basics are the workhorses of the kitchen, so always keep a few onions, white potatoes, sweet potatoes, and carrots on hand, as well as a head of garlic.

➥ Convenience foods make cooking easy. As well as the usual canned tomatoes, canned beans, etc., mentioned above, shortcut pantry ingredients such as fat-free marinara sauce, bottled salsas, vacuum-packed gnocchi, prebaked pizza crusts, and precooked rice and grains are must-haves for creating quick weeknight meals.

➥ Nuts are great flavor, texture, and nutrient enhancers, and just a sprinkle of chopped almonds, walnuts, pine nuts, or peanuts can take a dish to a new level of flavor. Buy nuts in small quantities, and if storing for longer than a couple of months, pop them in the freezer. Keep portions small, because all nuts are high in SmartPoints.

stock the refrigerator

You usually have basics such as low-fat or fat-free milk, yogurt, and cheese; eggs; mustard; ketchup; light mayo; and low-fat salad dressings on hand, but other foods should have a permanent home in the fridge, too.

➥ Quick-cooking vegetables are often used in the recipes in this book, and they can double as fast side dishes. Buy a few of these each week: asparagus, baby carrots, bell peppers, broccoli, Brussels sprouts, cauliflower, green beans, kale, snow peas, spinach, yellow squash, and zucchini. For serving suggestions, see "Quick-Cooking Veggies for 0 SmartPoints value" on page xv. To save time, buy pre-prepped veggies such as trimmed green beans and prewashed kale and spinach.

➡ Pump up flavor with fresh lemons and limes (use the zest and the juice), fresh ginger, and jalapeños or other chiles. These ingredients last a week or longer and can add robust flavor to almost any dish you cook.

➡ Keep a selection of fresh 0 SmartPoints value fruits to incorporate into salads and main dishes, and for snacks throughout the day. Refrigerated apples, pears, and citrus fruits are all long-keeping, delicious for snacking, and versatile for cooking.

➡ Fresh herbs are expensive but their flavor adds a punch to foods that you'll never achieve with dried versions. Always keep parsley and one or two other favorite herbs on hand.

➡ Don't forget refrigerated convenience foods such as prepared reduced-fat pesto, salsa, reduced-fat shredded cheese, fresh pasta, prewashed salad greens, coleslaw mix, prepped butternut squash, and precooked lentils and beets.

stock the freezer

➡ Keeping a stash of frozen foods means fewer trips to the supermarket, and if you can buy in bulk when foods are on sale or when you visit a warehouse store, you'll save money. Meats, poultry, and seafood spoil quickly in the refrigerator, so depending on your meal plan for the week, buy a couple of items fresh for the first few days, and then rely on foods from the freezer for later in the week.

➡ Skinless boneless chicken breasts and thighs, turkey cutlets, steaks, pork chops, fish fillets, shrimp, and unsweetened fruits and unseasoned veggies are essential staples for your freezer. Filled pastas, such as ravioli and tortellini, are good to keep on hand for quick meals, too.

➡ Thaw frozen foods safely in the refrigerator overnight or, if you forget, use the defrost setting on your microwave and you'll be cooking in minutes.

2. SUNDAY STRATEGIES

A few hours on Sunday (or whatever day is convenient for you) can make every weeknight meal go smoothly. Use the following tips to plan your strategy:

plan your week

▶ Dinners out and other evening commitments mean you'll need to look at your family's schedule each week before mapping out menus and shopping. When you decide how many dinners you'll be making for the week, select the recipes you want to make for each day.

▶ Make a shopping list based on the dishes you've chosen. To save searching the pantry multiple times, put a question mark by items you aren't sure whether you need to buy. Then check your pantry, refrigerator, and freezer to finalize your list.

▶ Find out if your supermarket has an app. Depending on the store, an app will allow you to make shopping lists, scan bar codes at home to add foods to your list, find out about sales, and add coupons to your account.

▶ Make planned leftovers part of your week. Look for the Double Duty tips throughout the book for suggestions on doubling a recipe or part of a recipe to streamline another meal.

▶ Most recipes in this book serve four, but if you're cooking for only two people, go ahead and make the entire recipe and enjoy the leftovers for lunch or for dinner later in the week.

▶ Round out your meals. Make fresh salads, quick-cooking vegetables, and grains part of your meals, too. Many of the recipes in this book have ideas for what to serve alongside, but for more inspiration see "Don't Sweat the Sides" on pages xiv-xv.

shop smart

▶ Go to the grocery store at an off time. On weekends, to avoid crowds and shop when the stores are most likely to be well stocked, go as early in the day as possible.

▶ Organize your list by the aisles at your store. Whether your list is digital or on paper, make sure it follows the order of the aisles so you don't waste time backtracking.

▶ Check yourself out. Skip waiting in line and use the ordinarily less popular self-checkout lanes. You'll save time and escape the frustration of standing in line.

get a head start

▶ Pre-prep your veggies. Chop onions, carrots, and other vegetables that you'll be using over the week. Wash and prep vegetables such as broccoli, green beans, or zucchini so they are steamer-ready when needed. If you prep you own salad greens and make your own dressings, do this on the weekend, too.

▶ Make a meal or two on the weekend. Some dishes taste great as a leftover. Get a step ahead on the week and cook Turkey and White Bean Chili, page 70, Southwestern Chicken Soup, page 150, or Curried Red Lentil and Pumpkin Soup, page 167.

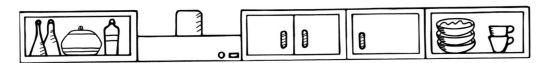

3. ORGANIZE THE KITCHEN

Even with a well-stocked pantry and the easiest recipes, if your kitchen is a jumbled mess, cooking will be stressful and take more time. Have a critical look around your kitchen and see which of these tips might make you a more efficient cook.

declutter equipment

➡ If you don't use it, give it to someone who will. Whittle down your kitchen equipment to what you actually put to work. If you have multiples of tools, consider downsizing to the number you might need at one time. Also think about ditching extraneous tools if a knife can perform the same function—out with the avocado slicer and the corn kernel remover. Donate the excess to a charity thrift shop.

➡ Put seldom-used equipment that you want to keep on a top shelf. If your kitchen storage area is limited, put these items in another room, in the garage, or in attic storage areas. This is the perfect solution for storing holiday cookie cutters, specialty cake pans, and very large pots, pans, or serving platters used for entertaining.

➡ Make cooking convenient. Most recipes in this book require only a skillet, saucepan, baking sheet, or roasting pan. Store these and other essential items as close as possible to the stove.

downsize and organize ingredients

➡ Clear out your pantry. Take away the opportunity for temptation by eliminating cookies, snack chips, and desserts to make room for healthier fare. The same goes for food gifts you'll never eat, condiments you thought you'd like but didn't, and foods you'll never take the time to make (bye-bye, croquembouche kit!). Donate unopened, unexpired items to a food bank or give them to friends or neighbors.

➡ Keep the six or eight spices you use most often, as well as salt and pepper, in a small bin near your food prep area. This saves time by eliminating the need to look through a large number of spice bottles all the time.

➡ Place frequently used items, such as olive oil, vinegar, pasta, and canned broths and tomatoes front and center on your pantry shelves. Move items used less often to top or bottom shelves.

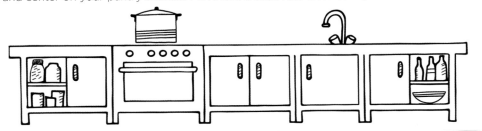

Summer Cobb Salad, 176

4. DON'T SWEAT THE SIDES

Once you've got the main dish under way, it's time to consider a side dish or two to go with your meal. Sides should be supersimple during the week: a salad of greens with fruits or veggies, steamed, microwaved, or stir-fried veggies, and/or a simply cooked grain or pasta. Don't forget the toaster oven—it's perfect for roasting a small amount of vegetables in 30 minutes or less. Here's how to make sides simple, and simply good for you.

simple salads

A fresh salad at dinner is a great way to get more fruits and veggies into your day. And it doesn't have to be complicated. Use packaged salad greens, easily prepped veggies and fruits, and premade low-fat dressings (or a few shakes of good olive oil and fresh lemon juice or vinegar), and you can put one of these salads together in about five minutes.

SPINACH AND STRAWBERRY SALAD
Toss together **baby spinach**, sliced fresh **strawberries,** thinly sliced **red onion,** and **fat-free raspberry vinaigrette dressing** (1 tablespoon fat-free raspberry vinaigrette dressing has 1 SmartPoints value).

KALE AND APPLE SALAD
Toss together **baby kale, apple** slices, and **fat-free balsamic vinaigrette dressing** (1 tablespoon fat-free balsamic vinaigrette dressing has 0 SmartPoints value). Sprinkle each serving with 1 tablespoon **slivered almonds** for an additional 1 SmartPoints value.

ORANGE AND FENNEL SALAD
Peel and slice **oranges** into rounds and arrange on a platter; sprinkle with thinly sliced **fennel** and chopped **fresh parsley,** and drizzle with **olive oil** and **vinegar** (1 teaspoon olive oil has 1 SmartPoints value).

ASIAN CABBAGE AND SNOW PEA SALAD
Toss together preshredded **cabbage,** trimmed and thinly sliced **snow peas,** and **light sesame ginger dressing** (1 tablespoon light sesame ginger dressing has 1 SmartPoints value). Sprinkle each serving with 1 tablespoon chopped peanuts for an additional 2 SmartPoints value.

CUCUMBER AND TOMATO SALAD
Toss together peeled and sliced **cucumbers,** quartered **plum tomatoes,** thinly sliced **red onion,** and chopped **fresh basil.** To make 4 servings of salad dressing, whisk together 2 tablespoons **red-wine vinegar,** 1 tablespoon **extra-virgin olive oil,** 1 tablespoon **chicken broth,** and **salt** and **black pepper** to taste (1 tablespoon of the dressing has 1 SmartPoints value). Sprinkle each serving with 1 tablespoon **feta** for an additional 1 SmartPoints value.

BABY GREENS AND GRAPES

Toss together **mixed baby greens** and halved seedless **grapes.** To make 4 servings of salad dressing, whisk together 4 teaspoons **extra-virgin olive oil,** 2 tablespoons **lemon juice,** and **salt** and **black pepper** to taste (2½ teaspoons of the dressing has 1 SmartPoints value). Sprinkle each serving with 1 tablespoon grated **Parmesan** for an additional 1 SmartPoints value.

quick-cooking veggies for 0 smartpoints value

Steaming, microwaving, or stir-frying veggies are the quickest and easiest ways to cook them. Your best bets for fast weeknight meals are asparagus, baby carrots, bell peppers, broccoli, Brussels sprouts, cauliflower, green beans, kale, snow peas, spinach, yellow squash, and zucchini. Any of these vegetables can be cooked in five minutes or less.

To pump up the flavor of cooked veggies, toss them with lemon juice, salt, and black pepper. Grated lemon, lime, or orange zest; chopped fresh herbs; balsamic vinegar; soy sauce; and butter, extra-virgin olive oil, or dark (Asian) sesame oil (½ teaspoon butter, 1 teaspoon olive oil, and 1 teaspoon sesame oil all have 1 SmartPoints value each) all make flavorful additions, too.

superfast grains, pastas, and polenta

While the main dish cooks, you can easily make one of these quick sides. Follow the package directions for cooking, but all the options in the list below will be ready in 15 minutes or less. For sides you don't even have to cook, look for precooked rice and grain blends at the supermarket next to the dry rice or in the frozen foods department.

To dress up plain grains and pastas, stir in salt and black pepper as well as grated lemon, lime, or orange zest; chopped fresh herbs; or butter, extra-virgin olive oil, or dark (Asian) sesame oil (½ teaspoon butter, 1 teaspoon olive oil, and 1 teaspoon sesame oil all have 1 SmartPoints value each).

- **Boil-in-bag white rice** (SmartPoints value per ½ cup: 3)
- **Instant white rice** (SmartPoints value per ½ cup: 3)
- **Bulgur** (SmartPoints value per ½ cup: 2)
- **Quick-cooking barley** (SmartPoints value per ½ cup: 3)
- **Quinoa** (SmartPoints value per ½ cup: 3)
- **Couscous** (SmartPoints value per ½ cup: 2)
- **Orzo, angel hair pasta, and rotini** (SmartPoints value per ½ cup: 3)
- **Fresh pasta** (SmartPoints value per ½ cup: 4)
- **Rice noodles** (SmartPoints value per ½ cup: 3)
- **Instant polenta** (SmartPoints value per ½ cup: 4)

chapter 1

EVERYONE'S FAVE:
CHICKEN

ROSEMARY CHICKEN WITH BALSAMIC-GLAZED ONIONS

serves 4   *gluten free*

4 (5-ounce) skinless boneless chicken breasts

1½ teaspoons minced fresh rosemary

½ teaspoon salt

¼ teaspoon black pepper

3 teaspoons olive oil

3 small onions, each cut into 8 wedges

¼ cup balsamic vinegar

2 tablespoons honey

2 teaspoons Worcestershire sauce

 1 Sprinkle chicken with rosemary, salt, and pepper. Heat 2 teaspoons oil in large skillet over medium-high heat. Add chicken and cook, turning once, until cooked through, about 8 minutes. Transfer to plate and keep warm.

2 Add remaining 1 teaspoon oil to skillet. Add onions and cook, covered, stirring occasionally, until tender and golden, about 10 minutes. Add vinegar, honey, and Worcestershire sauce and cook until onion mixture is syrupy, about 2 minutes. Serve onions with chicken.

6 SmartPoints value

Per serving (1 chicken breast and scant ½ cup onions): 266 Cal, 7 g Total Fat, 1 g Sat Fat, 388 mg Sod, 17 g Total Carb, 14 g Sugar, 1 g Fib, 32 g Prot.

cook's tip

Serve the chicken with a side of 0 SmartPoints veggies, such as green beans, broccoli, or asparagus.

GRILLED CHICKEN AND CORN SALAD WITH YOGURT-LIME DRESSING

serves 4   *gluten free*

¼ cup plain low-fat yogurt

¼ cup lime juice

1 tablespoon olive oil

1 teaspoon ground coriander

1 teaspoon salt

¼ teaspoon chili powder

¼ teaspoon grated lime zest

Pinch cayenne

2 large ears corn on the cob, shucked

4 (5-ounce) skinless boneless chicken breasts

1 pint cherry tomatoes, halved

1 small red onion, thinly sliced

1 cup fresh cilantro leaves

8 Boston lettuce leaves

1 Spray grill rack with nonstick spray. Preheat grill to medium-high or prepare medium-high fire.

2 To make dressing, whisk together yogurt, lime juice, oil, coriander, ½ teaspoon salt, chili powder, lime zest, and cayenne in large bowl. Let stand at room temperature.

3 Place corn on grill rack and grill, turning often, until softened and browned, 15–17 minutes. Meanwhile, sprinkle chicken with remaining ½ teaspoon salt. Place chicken on grill rack and grill, turning often, until chicken is cooked through, 8–10 minutes.

4 Transfer chicken and corn to cutting board. When cool enough to handle, shred chicken and cut kernels from corn. Add chicken, corn, tomatoes, onion, and cilantro to dressing and toss to combine. Divide lettuce among 4 plates and top evenly with chicken salad.

 6 SmartPoints value **Per serving** (1¾ cups salad and 2 lettuce leaves): 302 Cal, 9 g Total Fat, 2 g Sat Fat, 767 mg Sod, 24 g Total Carb, 9 g Sugar, 4 g Fib, 34 g Prot.

cook's tip

If you don't have fresh corn, you can use 1¾ cups thawed frozen corn kernels in this recipe.

CHICKEN WITH ROASTED RED BELL PEPPER—BASIL SAUCE

 serves 4 gluten free under 20 minutes

1 (7-ounce) jar roasted red peppers (not oil-packed), drained

1 tablespoon balsamic vinegar

1 garlic clove, chopped

¾ teaspoon salt

4 tablespoons chopped fresh basil

4 (5-ounce) skinless boneless chicken breasts

¼ teaspoon black pepper

Pinch cayenne

2 teaspoons olive oil

1 To make sauce, puree roasted peppers, vinegar, garlic, and ¼ teaspoon salt in blender or food processor. Scrape mixture into small saucepan and set over medium heat. Cook, stirring frequently, until sauce just begins to simmer. Remove from heat and stir in 2 tablespoons basil. Keep warm.

2 Meanwhile, sprinkle chicken with remaining 2 tablespoons basil, remaining ½ teaspoon salt, black pepper, and cayenne. Heat oil in large skillet over medium heat. Add chicken and cook, turning once, until browned and cooked through, 8–10 minutes. Slice chicken and serve with sauce.

3 SmartPoints value

Per serving (1 chicken breast and 2 tablespoons sauce): 203 Cal, 6 g Total Fat, 1 g Sat Fat, 696 mg Sod, 7 g Total Carb, 2 g Sugar, 0 g Fib, 30 g Prot.

double duty

Make extra roasted red pepper sauce and serve it later in the week with baked fish or grilled shrimp, or toss with pasta and vegetables.

Chicken with Roasted Red
Bell Pepper–Basil Sauce

Chicken with Cherry Tomato–Basil Sauce

CHICKEN WITH CHERRY TOMATO— BASIL SAUCE

serves 4 · *gluten free* · *under 20 minutes*

4 (5-ounce) skinless boneless chicken breasts

½ teaspoon salt

¼ teaspoon black pepper

2 teaspoons olive oil

1 large shallot, minced

2 garlic cloves, minced

1 pint cherry tomatoes, halved

¼ cup reduced-sodium chicken broth

¼ cup chopped fresh basil

1 Sprinkle chicken with salt and pepper. Heat oil in large nonstick skillet over medium heat. Add chicken and cook, turning once, until browned and cooked through, 8–10 minutes. Transfer chicken to platter and keep warm.

2 Add shallot and garlic to skillet. Cook, stirring often, until softened, about 2 minutes. Add tomatoes and broth and cook, stirring occasionally, until tomatoes begin to soften, about 4 minutes longer. Stir in basil. Spoon sauce over chicken.

Per serving (1 chicken breast and about ½ cup sauce): 206 Cal, 6 g Total Fat, 1 g Sat Fat, 485 mg Sod, 6 g Total Carb, 2 g Sugar, 1 g Fib, 31 g Prot.

cook's tip

To complete the meal, serve the chicken with a side of quinoa (½ cup cooked quinoa per serving will increase the SmartPoints value by 3).

BARBECUE RANCH CHICKEN SALAD

serves 4 • *gluten free*

½ cup tomato sauce

1 tablespoon honey mustard

1 tablespoon barbecue seasoning blend

2 teaspoons dark brown sugar

1 teaspoon onion powder

½ teaspoon Worcestershire sauce

4 (5-ounce) skinless boneless chicken breasts

½ teaspoon kosher salt

¼ teaspoon black pepper

6 cups chopped romaine lettuce

2 cups grape tomatoes, halved

1 red bell pepper, chopped

½ cup canned black beans, rinsed and drained

½ cup canned corn kernels, rinsed and drained

¼ cup reduced-fat ranch dressing

¼ cup crumbled soft goat cheese

¼ cup chopped scallions

1 Stir together tomato sauce, honey mustard, barbecue seasoning, brown sugar, onion powder, and Worcestershire sauce in small bowl. Set aside.

2 Heat ridged grill pan over medium-high heat. Sprinkle chicken with salt and black pepper. Place chicken in grill pan and cook, turning once, until almost done, about 6 minutes. Brush chicken with tomato-sauce mixture and cook, turning and brushing with sauce, until cooked through, about 2 minutes longer. Transfer chicken to cutting board and cut into slices.

3 Meanwhile, divide lettuce evenly among 4 plates. Top evenly with tomatoes, bell pepper, black beans, and corn. Top each salad with 1 chicken breast, drizzle evenly with dressing, and sprinkle evenly with goat cheese and scallions.

 8 SmartPoints value

Per serving (1 salad): 348 Cal, 11 g Total Fat, 4 g Sat Fat, 959 mg Sod, 27 g Total Carb, 11 g Sugar, 6 g Fib, 38 g Prot.

double duty

Make an extra batch of the grilled chicken to use for BBQ chicken sandwiches later in the week.

*Barbecue Ranch
Chicken Salad*

CHICKEN WITH PASTA AND PUTTANESCA SAUCE

serves 4

- 4 ounces whole wheat penne
- ½ cup seasoned dried bread crumbs
- 1 large egg
- 4 (5-ounce) thin-sliced skinless boneless chicken breast cutlets
- 2 teaspoons olive oil
- 6 plum tomatoes, diced
- 3 anchovy fillets, minced
- 2 garlic cloves, minced
- 1½ tablespoons drained capers
- 1 teaspoon balsamic vinegar
- ¼ teaspoon red pepper flakes

1 Cook penne according to package directions. Drain and keep warm.

2 Meanwhile, place bread crumbs on sheet of wax paper. Beat egg lightly in large shallow bowl or pie plate. Dip chicken into egg; then coat on both sides with bread crumbs, pressing lightly to adhere.

3 Heat oil in 12-inch nonstick skillet over medium heat. Add chicken and cook, turning once, until browned and cooked through, 6–8 minutes. Transfer to platter and keep warm.

4 Add tomatoes, anchovies, garlic, capers, vinegar, and red pepper flakes to skillet. Increase heat to medium-high and cook, stirring occasionally, until tomatoes are softened, about 5 minutes. Spoon sauce over chicken and serve with pasta.

8 SmartPoints value — **Per serving** (1 cutlet, ½ cup sauce, and ½ cup pasta): 397 Cal, 10 g Total Fat, 2 g Sat Fat, 657 mg Sod, 39 g Total Carb, 7 g Sugar, 5 g Fib, 40 g Prot.

cook's tip

Quick-cooking thin-sliced chicken cutlets work best in this recipe to ensure that the chicken cooks through without burning the crumb coating.

GRILLED CHICKEN KEBABS WITH ORZO

1½ pounds skinless boneless chicken breasts, cut into 1½-inch chunks

2 zucchini, cut into ½-inch slices

1 large lemon, thinly sliced

2 tablespoons chopped fresh oregano

¾ teaspoon salt

½ plus ⅛ teaspoon freshly ground black pepper

1 cup orzo

½ cup plain reduced-fat Greek yogurt

2 tablespoons lemon juice

1 garlic clove, crushed through press

1 cup cherry tomatoes, halved

16 Kalamata olives, pitted and chopped

1 teaspoon olive oil

1 Spray grill rack with nonstick spray. Preheat grill to medium-high or prepare medium-high fire.

2 Thread chicken, zucchini, and lemon slices alternately onto 6 (12-inch) metal skewers (if using wooden skewers, soak in water 20 minutes prior to use to prevent charring). Sprinkle kebabs with 1 tablespoon oregano, ¼ teaspoon salt, and ¼ teaspoon pepper. Lightly spray kebabs with olive-oil nonstick spray.

3 Place kebabs on grill rack and grill, turning occasionally, until chicken is cooked through, about 8 minutes.

4 Meanwhile, cook orzo according to package directions.

5 To make sauce, stir together yogurt, lemon juice, garlic, ¼ teaspoon salt, and ⅛ teaspoon pepper in small bowl.

6 Drain orzo and transfer to large bowl. Stir in tomatoes, olives, oil, remaining 1 tablespoon oregano, remaining ¼ teaspoon salt, and remaining ¼ teaspoon pepper.

7 Divide orzo mixture evenly among 6 plates and top with 1 chicken kebab. Serve with yogurt sauce.

6 SmartPoints value **Per serving** (1 chicken kebab, generous ⅔ cup orzo mixture, and scant 2 tablespoons sauce): 297 Cal, 6 g Total Fat, 1 g Sat Fat, 431 mg Sod, 28 g Total Carb, 4 g Sugar, 2 g Fib, 33 g Prot.

*Chicken and Vegetable
Kebabs with Creamy Pesto*

CHICKEN AND VEGETABLE KEBABS WITH CREAMY PESTO

serves 4   *gluten free*

- 3 cups fresh basil leaves
- 3 tablespoons water
- 2 tablespoons lemon juice
- 2 teaspoons extra-virgin olive oil
- 2 garlic cloves
- ¼ teaspoon salt
- ⅛ teaspoon black pepper
- Pinch red pepper flakes
- 1 pound skinless boneless chicken breasts, cut into 16 pieces
- 1 large red bell pepper, cut into 16 pieces
- 1 zucchini, halved lengthwise, each half cut into 8 pieces
- 1 red onion, cut into 16 pieces
- 2 tablespoons light cream cheese (Neufchâtel)
- 2 tablespoons grated Parmesan

1 Spray grill rack with nonstick spray. Preheat grill to medium-high or prepare medium-high fire.

2 Puree basil, water, lemon juice, oil, garlic, salt, black pepper, and red pepper flakes in blender or food processor.

3 Transfer 2 tablespoons basil mixture to large bowl. Add chicken, bell pepper, zucchini, and onion to bowl and toss to coat.

4 Add cream cheese and Parmesan to mixture remaining in blender and puree. Transfer sauce to small bowl.

5 Thread chicken and vegetables onto 8 (12-inch) metal skewers (if using wooden skewers, soak in water 20 minutes prior to use to prevent charring). Place kebabs on grill rack and grill, turning occasionally, until chicken is cooked through, about 10 minutes. Serve kebabs with sauce.

4 SmartPoints value

Per serving (2 kebabs and 2 tablespoons sauce): 219 Cal, 8 g Total Fat, 3 g Sat Fat, 362 mg Sod, 9 g Total Carb, 4 g Sugar, 3 g Fib, 28 g Prot.

cook's tip

If you're in a hurry, place the chicken and vegetables in a grill basket or a grill topper to cook instead of threading them onto skewers.

CREAMY CHICKEN PAPRIKASH WITH FRESH DILL

 serves 4

1 pound skinless boneless chicken breasts, cut into ½-inch pieces

¾ teaspoon salt

¼ teaspoon black pepper

3 teaspoons olive oil

1 large onion, chopped

1 red bell pepper, thinly sliced

2 garlic cloves, minced

2 tablespoons paprika

2 tablespoons all-purpose flour

1 (14½-ounce) can diced tomatoes

1 cup reduced-sodium chicken broth

3 tablespoons light sour cream

2 tablespoons chopped fresh dill

1 Sprinkle chicken with ½ teaspoon salt and black pepper. Heat 2 teaspoons oil in large skillet over medium-high heat. Add chicken in two batches and cook, stirring occasionally, until browned and cooked through, 3–4 minutes. Transfer to plate.

2 Reduce heat to medium and add remaining 1 teaspoon oil to skillet. Add onion, bell pepper, and garlic and cook, stirring occasionally, until softened, about 5 minutes. Add paprika, flour, and remaining ¼ teaspoon salt and cook, stirring constantly, 1 minute. Add tomatoes and broth and cook, stirring to scrape up browned bits from bottom of pan, until mixture comes to simmer and thickens slightly, about 3 minutes.

3 Return chicken to skillet and cook until heated through, 1 minute. Remove from heat and stir in sour cream and dill.

 Per serving (1¼ cups): 242 Cal, 8 g Total Fat, 2 g Sat Fat, 830 mg Sod, 15 g Total Carb, 5 g Sugar, 3 g Fib, 27 g Prot.

 **cook's tip**

Fresh dill is the traditional herb used in paprikash, but if it is not available, you can omit it or substitute chopped fresh parsley. The recipe will still be delicious.

CHICKEN AND VEGETABLE FRIED RICE

 serves 4 under 20 minutes

3 teaspoons canola oil

2 large eggs, lightly beaten

3 scallions, thinly sliced

2 large garlic cloves, minced

2 teaspoons minced peeled fresh ginger

1 red bell pepper, diced

¼ pound snow peas, trimmed and halved

1½ cups diced cooked skinless chicken breast

1 (8.8-ounce) package cooked brown rice (about 1¾ cups)

3 tablespoons reduced-sodium soy sauce

1 teaspoon Asian (dark) sesame oil

2 tablespoons chopped fresh cilantro

1 Heat 1 teaspoon oil in medium nonstick skillet over medium heat. Add eggs and cook, stirring, until firm, about 2 minutes. Transfer to plate.

2 Heat remaining 2 teaspoons oil in large, deep heavy skillet or wok over high heat. Add scallions, garlic, and ginger and stir-fry just until fragrant, about 15 seconds. Add bell pepper and snow peas and stir-fry until crisp-tender, about 2 minutes. Add chicken and stir-fry 30 seconds. Add rice and stir-fry until heated through, about 1 minute. Remove from heat and add eggs, stirring to break into small pieces. Stir in soy sauce and sesame oil.

3 Divide evenly among 4 plates and sprinkle with cilantro.

 Per serving (about 1½ cups): 333 Cal, 10 g Total Fat, 2 g Sat Fat, 488 mg Sod, 34 g Total Carb, 7 g Sugar, 7 g Fib, 27 g Prot.

 *cook's tip*

Use purchased rotisserie chicken breast or leftover chicken or turkey breast for this recipe.

CHICKEN SAUTÉ WITH BELL PEPPERS AND GOAT CHEESE

 serves 4

1½ tablespoons all-purpose flour

¼ teaspoon salt

¼ teaspoon black pepper

¾ pound skinless boneless chicken breasts, cut into 1-inch pieces

2 teaspoons extra-virgin olive oil

2 different-color bell peppers, thinly sliced

1 onion, thinly sliced

2 garlic cloves, minced

1 (8-ounce) can tomato sauce

¼ cup water

¼ cup thinly sliced fresh basil

4 tablespoons crumbled soft goat cheese

1 Mix together flour, salt, and black pepper on sheet of wax paper. Coat chicken with flour mixture.

2 Heat 1 teaspoon oil in large skillet over medium-high heat. Add chicken and cook, stirring occasionally, until browned and cooked through, about 6 minutes. Transfer to plate.

3 Add remaining 1 teaspoon oil to skillet. Add bell peppers and onion and cook, stirring occasionally, until tender, about 12 minutes. Add garlic and cook, stirring constantly, until fragrant, about 30 seconds.

4 Stir in tomato sauce and water and bring to simmer, stirring to scrape up any browned bits from bottom of skillet.

5 Return chicken and any accumulated juices to skillet and cook until heated through, 1 minute. Remove from heat and stir in basil.

6 Divide evenly among 4 plates and sprinkle evenly with goat cheese.

 Per serving (1 cup chicken mixture and 1 tablespoon cheese): 219 Cal, 9 g Total Fat, 4 g Sat Fat, 614 mg Sod, 12 g Total Carb, 5 g Sugar, 3 g Fib, 23 g Prot.

Chicken Sauté with Bell Peppers and Goat Cheese

Thai Ginger Chicken Burgers

THAI GINGER CHICKEN BURGERS

serves 4

1 pound ground skinless chicken breast

⅓ cup fat-free egg substitute

⅓ cup chopped fresh cilantro

¼ cup plus 2 tablespoons plain dried bread crumbs

4 scallions, white part only, chopped

1 teaspoon grated peeled fresh ginger

½ teaspoon grated lime zest

½ teaspoon salt

¼ teaspoon black pepper

2 teaspoons canola oil

4 multigrain hamburger buns, toasted

4 teaspoons Sriracha mayonnaise

16 thin slices English (seedless) cucumber

4 thin slices red onion

4 leaf lettuce leaves

1 Combine chicken, egg substitute, cilantro, ¼ cup bread crumbs, scallions, ginger, lime zest, salt, and pepper in large bowl just until blended.

2 Place remaining 2 tablespoons bread crumbs on sheet of wax paper. With damp hands, form chicken mixture into 4 (½-inch-thick) patties. Dredge patties in bread crumbs, pressing gently to coat.

3 Heat oil in large nonstick skillet over medium heat. Add patties. Cook, covered, turning occasionally, until instant-read thermometer inserted into side of burger registers 165°F, about 12 minutes.

4 Spread 1 teaspoon mayonnaise on cut side of each bun top. Serve burgers in buns with cucumber, onion, and lettuce.

Per serving (1 burger): 371 Cal, 11 g Total Fat, 2 g Sat Fat, 707 mg Sod, 34 g Total Carb, 7 g Sugar, 4 g Fib, 35 g Prot.

cook's tip

If you like spicy foods, try topping the burgers with a small amount of sambal oelek, a spicy chile-based condiment.

SOBA CHICKEN NOODLE BOWL

serves 6

6 ounces thin 100% buckwheat soba noodles

2 teaspoons canola oil

2 large garlic cloves, finely chopped

2 teaspoons grated peeled fresh ginger

¾ pound chicken tenders, cut into ¾-inch chunks

4 cups reduced-sodium chicken broth

2 cups water

1 (5-ounce) package sliced shiitake mushroom caps

¼ cup reduced-sodium soy sauce

½ cup snow peas, trimmed and cut diagonally into ½-inch-wide strips

½ cup thawed frozen baby peas

2 cups packed baby spinach

2 scallions, finely chopped

2 teaspoons Asian (dark) sesame oil

1 Cook noodles according to package directions. Drain and keep warm.

2 Meanwhile, heat oil in large Dutch oven over medium-high heat. Add garlic and ginger and cook, stirring constantly, until fragrant, 30 seconds. Add chicken and cook, stirring often, until chicken is no longer pink, 2 minutes.

3 Add broth, water, mushrooms, and soy sauce. Cover and bring to boil. Stir in snow peas, baby peas, and spinach and cook until snow peas are crisp-tender, about 2 minutes. Stir in noodles. Ladle soup evenly into 6 bowls. Sprinkle evenly with scallions and drizzle with sesame oil.

5 SmartPoints value® **Per serving** (about 2 cups): 225 Cal, 5 g Total Fat, 1 g Sat Fat, 951 mg Sod, 27 g Total Carb, 2 g Sugar, 2 g Fib, 18 g Prot.

cook's tip

Look for thin soba buckwheat noodles in the Asian aisle of supermarkets and natural food stores or in Asian grocers.

*Soba Chicken
Noodle Bowl*

ASIAN CHICKEN AND VEGGIE TORTILLA WRAPS

- 2 cups packaged coleslaw mix
- 4 scallions, thinly sliced
- ⅛ teaspoon red pepper flakes
- 1 cup finely chopped cooked skinless chicken breast or turkey breast
- 2 tablespoons chopped unsalted dry-roasted peanuts
- 2 tablespoons chopped fresh basil
- 2 tablespoons chopped fresh mint
- 4 teaspoons lime juice
- 2 teaspoons Asian (dark) sesame oil
- 2 teaspoons reduced-sodium soy sauce
- 2 (10-inch) burrito-size fat-free flour tortillas, warmed

1 Spray large skillet with nonstick spray and set over medium-high heat. Add coleslaw mix, scallions, and red pepper flakes and cook, stirring frequently, until cabbage begins to wilt, about 3 minutes.

2 Add chicken and cook, stirring frequently, until heated through, about 3 minutes. Remove from heat and stir in peanuts, basil, and mint.

3 Meanwhile, stir together lime juice, sesame oil, and soy sauce in small bowl.

4 Spoon filling evenly onto tortillas. Drizzle filling evenly with lime juice mixture and roll up. Cut wraps in half on slight diagonal. Serve at once.

 Per serving (½ wrap): 206 Cal, 5 g Total Fat, 1 g Sat Fat, 353 mg Sod, 17 g Total Carb, 3 g Sugar, 4 g Fib, 22 g Prot.

BRAISED CHICKEN WITH FETA AND OLIVES

serves 4  gluten free

1 teaspoon olive oil

4 (5-ounce) skinless boneless chicken thighs, trimmed

½ teaspoon salt

¼ teaspoon black pepper

1 small onion, halved and thinly sliced

½ cup reduced-sodium chicken broth

2 tomatoes, chopped

8 pitted Kalamata olives, chopped

3 tablespoons chopped fresh basil

4 tablespoons crumbled feta

1 Heat oil in large skillet over medium-high heat. Sprinkle chicken with salt and pepper. Add chicken to skillet and cook, turning once, until browned, about 8 minutes. Transfer to plate.

2 Add onion to skillet and cook, stirring occasionally, until it begins to soften, about 3 minutes. Stir in broth, tomatoes, and olives and bring to boil. Return chicken to skillet.

3 Reduce heat to low and simmer, covered, until vegetables are tender and chicken is cooked through, about 5 minutes. Remove skillet from heat and stir in basil.

4 Divide chicken and sauce evenly among 4 plates. Sprinkle evenly with feta.

 Per serving (1 chicken thigh, ½ cup sauce, and 1 tablespoon feta): 370 Cal, 27 g Total Fat, 8 g Sat Fat, 615 mg Sod, 6 g Total Carb, 3 g Sugar, 1 g Fib, 32 g Prot.

cook's tip

You can use fresh dill or mint instead of basil in this recipe if you prefer.

Chicken Thighs with Ginger-Plum Sauce

CHICKEN THIGHS WITH GINGER-PLUM SAUCE

serves 4 　*gluten free*

- 4 (5-ounce) skinless boneless chicken thighs, trimmed
- ¼ teaspoon salt
- ¼ teaspoon black pepper
- 2 teaspoons canola oil
- 6 plums, pitted and sliced
- 1 tablespoon grated peeled fresh ginger
- 1 garlic clove, minced
- ¼ cup reduced-sodium chicken broth
- ¼ cup frozen apple juice concentrate, thawed

1 Sprinkle chicken with salt and pepper. Heat 1 teaspoon oil in large skillet over medium-high heat. Add chicken and cook, turning once, until browned, about 8 minutes. Transfer chicken to plate.

2 Add remaining 1 teaspoon oil to skillet. Add plums, ginger, and garlic and cook, stirring often, until plums are softened, 2–3 minutes. Add broth to skillet and bring to boil over high heat, scraping up any browned bits from bottom of pan. Stir in apple juice concentrate.

3 Return chicken to skillet. Reduce heat and simmer, covered, until chicken is cooked through, about 5 minutes.

6 SmartPoints value — **Per serving** (1 chicken thigh and about ½ cup sauce): 269 Cal, 8 g Total Fat, 2 g Sat Fat, 311 mg Sod, 19 g Total Carb, 17 g Sugar, 2 g Fib, 29 g Prot.

cook's tip

To save time, prep the plums, ginger, and garlic while the chicken browns.

SAUTÉED CHICKEN WITH LEMON-CAPER SAUCE

 serves 4 *under 20 minutes*

¼ cup all-purpose flour

¼ teaspoon black pepper

4 (5-ounce) skinless boneless chicken thighs, trimmed

2 teaspoons olive oil

1 cup reduced-sodium chicken broth

2 tablespoons lemon juice

1½ tablespoons drained capers

Chopped fresh parsley

1 Combine flour and pepper on sheet of wax paper. Coat chicken with flour mixture.

2 Heat oil in large skillet over medium heat. Add chicken to skillet and cook, turning once, until browned and cooked through, about 10 minutes. Transfer to plate.

3 Add broth to skillet and bring to boil, stirring to scrape up browned bits from bottom of pan. Cook until broth is reduced slightly, about 3 minutes. Return chicken to skillet. Reduce heat to low and simmer, covered, until chicken is heated through, about 2 minutes. Stir in lemon juice and capers. Sprinkle with parsley.

4 Divide chicken evenly among 4 plates. Drizzle with sauce.

5 SmartPoints value **Per serving** (1 chicken thigh and 1½ tablespoons sauce): 226 Cal, 8 g Total Fat, 2 g Sat Fat, 329 mg Sod, 7 g Total Carb, 1 g Sugar, 0 g Fib, 29 g Prot.

cook's tip

Linguine or fettuccine makes a perfect accompaniment to this saucy dish (¾ cup cooked whole wheat or regular pasta per serving will increase the SmartPoints value by 4).

Sautéed Chicken with
Lemon-Caper Sauce

*Stir-Fried Chicken
with Vegetables*

STIR-FRIED CHICKEN WITH VEGETABLES

serves 2   *under 20 minutes*

- 2 teaspoons plus 1 tablespoon dry or sweet sherry
- 2 teaspoons plus 1 tablespoon reduced-sodium soy sauce
- 2 teaspoons cornstarch
- ½ pound skinless boneless chicken thighs, trimmed and cut into ½-inch pieces
- 2 tablespoons reduced-sodium chicken broth
- 1 tablespoon hoisin sauce
- 1 tablespoon chili-garlic sauce
- 3 teaspoons canola oil
- 3 garlic cloves, crushed with flat side of knife
- 1 large yellow bell pepper, thinly sliced
- 1 cup cherry tomatoes, halved
- ¼ teaspoon salt

1 Whisk together 2 teaspoons sherry, 2 teaspoons soy sauce, and cornstarch in medium bowl until smooth. Add chicken and stir to coat.

2 Stir together chicken broth, hoisin sauce, chili-garlic sauce, remaining 1 tablespoon soy sauce, and remaining 1 tablespoon sherry in small bowl. Set aside.

3 Heat wok or large skillet over high heat until drop of water sizzles in it. Add 1½ teaspoons oil and swirl to coat pan. Add garlic and stir-fry until fragrant, about 10 seconds. Push garlic to side of wok. Add chicken to wok and arrange in single layer. Cook without stirring 1 minute; then stir-fry until chicken is cooked through, about 1 minute longer.

4 Add remaining 1½ teaspoons oil to wok. Add bell pepper, tomatoes, and salt and stir-fry 30 seconds. Add reserved chicken-broth mixture to wok and stir-fry until bell pepper is crisp-tender, about 1 minute longer. Discard garlic.

 Per serving (1½ cups): 331 Cal, 12 g Total Fat, 2 g Sat Fat, 1,010 mg Sod, 23 g Total Carb, 10 g Sugar, 6 g Fib, 28 g Prot.

RED CURRY CHICKEN WITH CAULIFLOWER

 serves 4   gluten free

1 pound skinless boneless chicken thighs, trimmed and cut into 1½-inch pieces

¾ teaspoon salt

1 teaspoon canola oil

1 yellow bell pepper, thinly sliced

6 scallions, cut into 1-inch pieces

1 (14-ounce) can light (low-fat) coconut milk

1 (12-ounce) bag fresh cauliflower florets, cut into bite-size pieces

1 (6-ounce) bag shredded carrots

2½ teaspoons Thai red curry paste

2 teaspoons sugar

½ cup torn fresh basil leaves

2 teaspoons lime juice

1 Sprinkle chicken with ½ teaspoon salt. Heat ½ teaspoon oil in large skillet over medium-high heat. Add chicken and cook, turning occasionally, until browned and cooked through, about 7 minutes. Transfer chicken to plate.

2 Add remaining ½ teaspoon oil to skillet. Add bell pepper and scallions and cook, stirring often, until scallions turn bright green, about 3 minutes. Add coconut milk, cauliflower, carrots, curry paste, sugar, and remaining ¼ teaspoon salt and bring to boil. Reduce heat to low and simmer, covered, stirring occasionally, until vegetables are tender, about 6 minutes.

3 Return chicken to skillet and cook until heated through, about 1 minute. Remove skillet from heat and stir in basil and lime juice.

 6 SmartPoints value   **Per serving** (1½ cups): 285 Cal, 12 g Total Fat, 5 g Sat Fat, 670 mg Sod, 19 g Total Carb, 9 g Sugar, 5 g Fib, 26 g Prot.

 **cook's tip**   *Serve this saucy dish with rice noodles (¾ cup cooked white rice noodles per serving will increase the SmartPoints value by 4).*

CHICKEN SAUSAGES AND VEGETABLES OVER HERBED POLENTA

serves 4

1 teaspoon olive oil

1 (12-ounce) package cooked smoked Italian-style chicken sausages, sliced on diagonal into ½-inch slices

1 onion, halved lengthwise and sliced

1 yellow or red bell pepper, thinly sliced

1 (8-ounce) package cremini mushrooms, sliced

2 garlic cloves, minced

3⅓ cups reduced-sodium chicken broth

3 teaspoons chopped fresh rosemary

1 cup instant polenta

¼ cup plus 2 tablespoons freshly grated pecorino Romano

1 Heat oil in large skillet over medium-high heat. Add sausages and cook, turning once, until browned, about 5 minutes. Transfer sausages to plate and set aside.

2 Add onion, bell pepper, and mushrooms to skillet. Cook, covered, stirring occasionally, until vegetables begin to soften, about 5 minutes. Add garlic and cook, stirring constantly, until fragrant, 1 minute. Stir in ⅓ cup broth, 2 teaspoons rosemary, and sausages. Reduce heat and simmer, covered, until vegetables are tender, about 5 minutes.

3 Meanwhile, bring remaining 3 cups broth to boil in medium saucepan over medium-high heat. Add remaining 1 teaspoon rosemary. Gradually whisk in polenta. Reduce heat and cook, whisking constantly, until thick and creamy, about 1 minute. Remove from heat and stir in ¼ cup pecorino.

4 Divide polenta evenly among 4 plates. Top evenly with sausage mixture and sprinkle evenly with remaining 2 tablespoons pecorino.

9 SmartPoints value

Per serving (¾ cup polenta, about 1 cup sausage and vegetable mixture, and ½ tablespoon cheese): 330 Cal, 10 g Total Fat, 3 g Sat Fat, 1,065 mg Sod, 38 g Total Carb, 5 g Sugar, 5 g Fib, 20 g Prot.

chapter 2

PROTEIN POWER:
STEAKS & CHOPS

STEAK WITH FRESH TOMATO AND CORN SALSA

- 1 (1-pound) boneless lean sirloin steak (1 inch thick), trimmed
- ½ teaspoon ground cumin
- ½ teaspoon salt
- ¼ teaspoon black pepper
- 1 teaspoon canola oil
- 1 ear corn on the cob, shucked
- 1 cup cherry or grape tomatoes, quartered
- ½ red onion, diced
- 1 jalapeño pepper, seeded and minced
- 1 tablespoon lime juice
- ¼ cup chopped fresh cilantro

1 Sprinkle steak with cumin, ¼ teaspoon salt, and black pepper. Heat oil in large heavy skillet over medium-high heat. Place steak in skillet and cook, turning once, until instant-read thermometer inserted into side of steak registers 145°F, about 8 minutes. Transfer to cutting board and let stand 5 minutes.

2 Meanwhile, wrap corn in paper towel and microwave on High 5 minutes. Rinse under cold running water until cool. Cut kernels from cob into medium bowl. Add tomatoes, onion, jalapeño, lime juice, cilantro, and remaining ¼ teaspoon salt.

3 Cut steak into 12 slices. Serve with salsa.

 Per serving (3 slices steak and ½ cup salsa): 191 Cal, 6 g Total Fat, 2 g Sat Fat, 363 mg Sod, 9 g Total Carb, 3 g Sugar, 2 g Fib, 27 g Prot.

 *Turn the steak and salsa into tacos by serving them in corn tortillas (2 medium corn tortillas per serving will increase the SmartPoints value by 4).*

Steak with Fresh Tomato
and Corn Salsa

PEPPERED SIRLOIN WITH BLACK BEAN AND AVOCADO SALAD

serves 4   *gluten free*   *under 20 minutes* 🕐

- 1 (1-pound) boneless lean sirloin steak (1 inch thick), trimmed
- ¾ teaspoon salt
- ¾ teaspoon black pepper
- 1 (15½-ounce) can black beans, rinsed and drained
- 1 cup frozen corn kernels, thawed
- 12 grape tomatoes, quartered
- ½ avocado, pitted, peeled, and cut into ½-inch pieces
- 1 jalapeño pepper, seeded and minced
- 2 tablespoons lime juice
- 2 teaspoons olive oil
- 3 tablespoons chopped fresh cilantro

Lime wedges

1 Sprinkle steak with ½ teaspoon salt and black pepper. Spray ridged grill pan with nonstick spray and set over medium-high heat. Place steak in pan and cook, turning once, until instant-read thermometer inserted into side of steak registers 145°F, about 8 minutes. Transfer to cutting board and let stand 5 minutes.

2 Meanwhile, to make salad, toss together beans, corn, tomatoes, avocado, jalapeño, lime juice, oil, cilantro, and remaining ¼ teaspoon salt in serving bowl.

3 Cut steak into 12 slices and serve with salad and lime wedges.

8 SmartPoints value

Per serving (3 slices steak and ¾ cup salad): 356 Cal, 11 g Total Fat, 3 g Sat Fat, 928 mg Sod, 32 g Total Carb, 4 g Sugar, 11 g Fib, 34 g Prot.

double duty

Make a double batch of the Black Bean and Avocado Salad and enjoy it over salad greens for lunch the next day.

GRILLED KOREAN STEAK IN LETTUCE CUPS

serves 4

- 1 (1-pound) boneless lean sirloin steak (1 inch thick), trimmed
- ½ teaspoon salt
- ½ teaspoon black pepper
- 2 tablespoons reduced-sodium soy sauce
- 2 teaspoons Asian (dark) sesame oil
- 2 teaspoons brown sugar
- 1 teaspoon lime juice
- 1 teaspoon grated peeled fresh ginger
- 1 teaspoon minced garlic
- ¼ teaspoon red pepper flakes
- 8 radishes, cut into matchstick strips
- 6 scallions
- 1 carrot, coarsely shredded
- 1 red bell pepper, very thinly sliced
- 16 large Bibb lettuce leaves
- 2 tablespoons toasted sesame seeds

Lime wedges

1 Sprinkle steak with salt and black pepper. Spray large ridged grill pan with nonstick spray and set over medium-high heat. Place steak in pan and cook, turning once, until instant-read thermometer inserted into side of steak registers 145°F, about 8 minutes. Transfer to cutting board and let stand 5 minutes.

2 Meanwhile, stir together soy sauce, sesame oil, brown sugar, lime juice, ginger, garlic, and red pepper flakes in small bowl.

3 Cut steak across grain into 12 thin slices. Divide steak, radishes, scallions, carrot, and bell pepper among lettuce leaves. Drizzle evenly with soy-sauce mixture and sprinkle with sesame seeds. Serve with lime wedges.

4 SmartPoints value — **Per serving** (4 filled lettuce cups): 231 Cal, 9 g Total Fat, 2 g Sat Fat, 630 mg Sod, 10 g Total Carb, 5 g Sugar, 3 g Fib, 28 g Prot.

cook's tip

To save time, look for toasted sesame seeds in the spice section at the supermarket. To toast your own, put the seeds in a small dry skillet and toast over medium heat, stirring constantly, until lightly browned and fragrant, about 3 minutes.

*Spice-Crusted Steak
with Wild Mushrooms*

SPICE-CRUSTED STEAK WITH WILD MUSHROOMS

 serves 4 *gluten free* *under 20 minutes*

- 1 (1-pound) boneless lean sirloin steak (1 inch thick), trimmed
- ¾ teaspoon salt
- ½ teaspoon coarsely ground black pepper
- ½ teaspoon ground coriander
- ½ teaspoon ground cumin
- 2 teaspoons olive oil
- 1 onion, thinly sliced
- 1 pound mixed wild mushrooms, sliced
- 2 teaspoons chopped fresh rosemary
- ¼ cup dry white wine

1 Sprinkle steak with ½ teaspoon salt, ¼ teaspoon pepper, coriander, and cumin. Heat 1 teaspoon oil in large heavy skillet over medium-high heat. Place steak in skillet and cook, turning once, until instant-read thermometer inserted into side of steak registers 145°F, about 8 minutes. Transfer to cutting board and let stand 5 minutes.

2 Meanwhile, heat remaining 1 teaspoon oil in another large skillet over medium-high heat. Add onion and cook, stirring, until softened, about 5 minutes. Add mushrooms and rosemary and cook, stirring, until mushrooms are browned, about 5 minutes. Add wine, remaining ¼ teaspoon salt, and remaining ¼ teaspoon pepper and cook, stirring, until mushrooms are tender, about 2 minutes longer.

3 Cut steak into 12 slices. Serve with mushrooms.

 Per serving (3 slices steak and ½ cup mushrooms): 236 Cal, 7 g Total Fat, 2 g Sat Fat, 526 mg Sod, 10 g Total Carb, 3 g Sugar, 3 g Fib, 31 g Prot.

 *cook's tip*

Look for packages of mixed wild mushrooms in the produce section at the supermarket. If they are not available, you can use any combination of mushrooms that you find.

HARISSA-SPICED SIRLOIN WITH MINT COUSCOUS

serves 4 *under 20 minutes*

2 tablespoons harissa

2 teaspoons olive oil

1 teaspoon dried oregano

½ teaspoon salt

1 (1-pound) boneless lean sirloin steak (1 inch thick), trimmed

1 cup reduced-sodium chicken broth

2 tablespoons lemon juice

1 cup whole wheat couscous

2 tablespoons golden raisins

2 tablespoons pine nuts, toasted

1 tablespoon chopped fresh mint

1 Combine harissa, 1 teaspoon oil, oregano, and ¼ teaspoon salt in small bowl. Spread over both sides of steak. Let stand at room temperature 10 minutes. Spray large ridged grill pan with nonstick spray and set over medium-high heat. Place steak in pan and cook, turning once, until instant-read thermometer inserted into side of steak registers 145°F, about 8 minutes. Transfer to cutting board and let stand 5 minutes.

2 Meanwhile, bring broth, lemon juice, remaining 1 teaspoon oil, and remaining ¼ teaspoon salt to boil in medium saucepan. Add couscous and raisins. Cover and remove from heat. Let stand 5 minutes; then fluff with fork. Stir in pine nuts and mint.

3 Cut steak across grain into 12 slices. Serve with couscous.

10 SmartPoints value **Per serving** (3 slices steak and ¾ cup couscous): 382 Cal, 11 g Total Fat, 3 g Sat Fat, 485 mg Sod, 39 g Total Carb, 6 g Sugar, 6 g Fib, 33 g Prot.

cook's tip

Harissa is a North African condiment made from chiles, cumin, garlic, and caraway seeds. It can be found in the ethnic section of most supermarkets. If you can't find it, you can use any type of chili paste in this recipe.

*Harissa-Spiced Sirloin
with Mint Couscous*

*Thai Beef and
Pea Shoot Salad*

THAI BEEF AND PEA SHOOT SALAD

serves 4 gluten free under 20 minutes

1 (1-pound) boneless lean sirloin steak (1 inch thick), trimmed

¾ teaspoon salt

2 tablespoons light brown sugar

2 tablespoons water

1 tablespoon rice vinegar

1 teaspoon Asian fish sauce

Grated zest and juice of 1 lime

1 carrot, cut into matchstick strips

1 small cucumber, seeded and cut into matchstick strips

¼ small jicama, cut into matchstick strips (about 2 ounces)

1 cup pea shoots

½ cup fresh cilantro leaves

1 Sprinkle steak with ½ teaspoon salt. Spray large ridged grill pan with nonstick spray and set over medium-high heat. Place steak in skillet and cook, turning once, until instant-read thermometer inserted into side of steak registers 145°F, about 8 minutes. Transfer to cutting board and let stand 5 minutes.

2 Meanwhile, to make salad, whisk together brown sugar, water, vinegar, fish sauce, lime zest and juice, and remaining ¼ teaspoon salt in large bowl. Add carrot, cucumber, jicama, pea shoots, and cilantro and toss to coat well.

3 Cut steak across grain into 12 slices. Serve steak with salad.

 Per serving (3 slices steak and 1½ cups salad): 195 Cal, 4 g Total Fat, 2 g Sat Fat, 630 mg Sod, 12 g Total Carb, 8 g Sugar, 2 g Fib, 26 g Prot.

cook's tip

Pea shoots are the tender leaves of the pea plant. They add fresh flavor and texture to any salad. If you can't find them, substitute mixed baby greens or baby spinach in this salad.

SIRLOIN AND ARUGULA SALAD WITH BALSAMIC VINAIGRETTE

serves 4 🏺 *gluten free* 🚫 *under 20 minutes* ⏱

- 1 (1-pound) boneless lean sirloin steak (1 inch thick), trimmed
- ¾ teaspoon salt
- ¼ plus ⅛ teaspoon black pepper
- 1 tablespoon olive oil
- 1 tablespoon balsamic vinegar
- 1 teaspoon Dijon mustard
- 1 teaspoon water
- 1 large shallot, minced
- 1 garlic clove, minced
- 8 cups loosely packed arugula
- 1 pint grape tomatoes, halved
- 1 cup roasted red peppers (not oil-packed), drained and chopped
- 2 tablespoons chopped fresh basil
- 2 tablespoons finely shredded Parmesan

1 Spray large ridged grill pan with nonstick spray and set over medium-high heat. Sprinkle steak with ½ teaspoon salt and ¼ teaspoon black pepper. Place steak in skillet and cook, turning once, until instant-read thermometer inserted into side of steak registers 145°F, about 8 minutes. Transfer to cutting board and let stand 5 minutes.

2 Meanwhile, whisk together oil, vinegar, mustard, water, remaining ¼ teaspoon salt, and remaining ⅛ teaspoon pepper in large bowl. Stir in shallot and garlic. Add arugula, tomatoes, roasted peppers, and basil and toss to coat.

3 Divide salad evenly among 4 plates and sprinkle with Parmesan. Cut steak across grain into 12 slices. Top salad with steak and serve at once.

 5 SmartPoints value

Per serving (3 slices steak and about 2 cups salad): 277 Cal, 11 g Total Fat, 3 g Sat Fat, 754 mg Sod, 19 g Total Carb, 8 g Sugar, 2 g Fib, 30 g Prot.

Make a double batch of this classic version of balsamic vinaigrette to serve on salads later in the week. It will keep in a covered container in the refrigerator up to a week.

BROILED STEAK AND PEPPERS WITH CREAMY SALSA VERDE

serves 4   *gluten free*   *under 20 minutes*

1½ teaspoons ground cumin

1 teaspoon dried oregano

½ teaspoon salt

2 yellow bell peppers, quartered

1 poblano pepper, quartered

1 (1-pound) lean flank steak, trimmed

1 cup fresh cilantro leaves

¾ cup fat-free salsa verde

2 tablespoons light sour cream

1 Preheat boiler. Spray broiler rack with nonstick spray.

2 Stir together cumin, oregano, and salt in small cup. Combine peppers in medium bowl and spray lightly with nonstick spray. Sprinkle peppers with half of seasoning mixture. Sprinkle steak with remaining seasoning. Arrange steak and peppers in single layer on prepared rack.

3 Broil 5 inches from heat, turning steak and peppers once, until peppers are crisp-tender and instant-read thermometer inserted into side of steak registers 145°F, about 8 minutes. Transfer steak to cutting board and let stand 5 minutes.

4 Meanwhile, to make sauce, puree cilantro, salsa, and sour cream in blender or food processor.

5 Cut steak across grain into 16 slices. Serve steak and peppers with sauce.

 Per serving (4 slices steak, 3 pieces pepper, and ¼ cup sauce): 210 Cal, 8 g Total Fat, 3 g Sat Fat, 577 mg Sod, 9 g Total Carb, 4 g Sugar, 3 g Fib, 27 g Prot.

Serve the steak and peppers with steamed baby potatoes (4 ounces cooked baby potatoes per serving will increase the SmartPoints value by 3).

GRILLED FLANK STEAK WITH CLEMENTINE SALAD

serves 4 *gluten free* *under 20 minutes*

1 (1-pound) lean flank steak, trimmed

¾ teaspoon salt

½ teaspoon chili powder

2 large clementines, peeled, sectioned, and cut into ½ inch pieces

¼ cup chopped fresh cilantro

1 jalapeño pepper, seeded and minced

2 tablespoons minced scallion

¼ cup orange juice

1 tablespoon balsamic vinegar

1 teaspoon canola oil

⅛ teaspoon black pepper

1 Spray large ridged grill pan with nonstick spray and set over medium-high heat. Sprinkle steak with ½ teaspoon salt and chili powder. Place steak in pan and cook, turning once, until instant-read thermometer inserted into side of steak registers 145°F, about 10 minutes. Transfer to cutting board and let stand 5 minutes.

2 Meanwhile, to make salad, stir together clementines, cilantro, jalapeño, and scallion in medium bowl.

3 To make dressing, whisk together orange juice, vinegar, oil, remaining ¼ teaspoon salt, and black pepper in small bowl.

4 Cut steak across grain into 16 slices and divide evenly among 4 plates. Top steak evenly with salad and drizzle evenly with dressing.

 Per serving (4 slices steak, ⅓ cup salad, and 1½ tablespoons dressing): 220 Cal, 8 g Total Fat, 2 g Sat Fat, 651 mg Sod, 12 g Total Carb, 9 g Sugar, 2 g Fib, 25 g Prot.

 *Serve the steak and salad over rice (½ cup cooked brown rice per serving will increase the SmartPoints value by 4).*

Grilled Flank Steak with
Clementine Salad

GRILLED FLANK STEAK WITH TOMATO-FENNEL SALAD

serves 4 🍽   *gluten free* 🚫

- 4 plum tomatoes, each cut into 6 wedges
- 2 tablespoons chopped fresh parsley
- 2 teaspoons grated lemon zest
- 1 tablespoon lemon juice
- 1½ teaspoons olive oil
- ¾ teaspoon salt
- ¼ teaspoon black pepper
- 1 (1-pound) lean flank steak, trimmed
- 1 fennel bulb, cut lengthwise into ½-inch-thick slices

1 Spray grill rack with nonstick spray. Preheat grill to medium-high or prepare medium-high fire.

2 Stir together tomatoes, parsley, lemon zest and juice, oil, ¼ teaspoon salt, and ⅛ teaspoon pepper in medium bowl. Set aside.

3 Sprinkle steak with remaining ½ teaspoon salt and remaining ⅛ teaspoon pepper. Lightly spray fennel with nonstick spray. Place steak and fennel on grill rack. Grill, turning fennel occasionally and steak once, until fennel is tender and instant-read thermometer inserted into center of steak registers 145°F, about 10 minutes.

4 Transfer steak to cutting board and let stand 5 minutes. Remove core from fennel and thinly slice. Stir fennel into tomato mixture. Cut steak into 12 slices and serve with salad.

Per serving: (3 slices steak and 1 cup salad): 219 Cal, 9 g Total Fat, 3 g Sat Fat, 538 mg Sod, 10 g Total Carb, 3 g Sugar, 3 g Fib, 26 g Prot.

cook's tip

If you're not a fan of the flavor of anise or licorice, don't let that stop you from trying fresh fennel. The flavor is quite mild, and in this colorful salad, it makes a perfect accompaniment to the richly flavored grilled steak.

FILETS MIGNONS WITH ORANGE AND AVOCADO SALAD

serves 4   **gluten free**   **under 20 minutes** 🕐

1 large navel orange

1 avocado, halved, pitted, peeled, and diced

1 scallion, thinly sliced

¼ cup diced red bell pepper

2 tablespoons chopped fresh basil

Pinch plus ½ teaspoon salt

Pinch cayenne

4 (¼-pound) filets mignons, trimmed

¾ teaspoon ground cumin

¼ teaspoon black pepper

1 teaspoon canola oil

 To make salad, grate 1 teaspoon zest from orange and place in medium bowl. With sharp knife, peel orange, removing all white pith. Chop orange, removing any seeds. Add orange to bowl. Add avocado, scallion, bell pepper, basil, pinch salt, and cayenne and toss to combine.

2 Sprinkle steak with remaining ½ teaspoon salt, cumin, and black pepper. Heat oil in large heavy skillet over medium-high heat. Place steaks in skillet and cook, turning once, until instant-read thermometer inserted into side of steaks registers 145°F, about 6 minutes. Serve steaks with salad.

5 SmartPoints value   **Per serving** (1 filet and ½ cup salad): 263 Cal, 13 g Total Fat, 3 g Sat Fat, 430 mg Sod, 10 g Total Carb, 5 g Sugar, 4 g Fib, 26 g Prot.

cook's tip

To use leftover basil, toss the whole basil leaves into a green salad for a fresh burst of herb flavor.

Steak and Pepper Sandwiches with Chipotle Mayo

STEAK AND PEPPER SANDWICHES WITH CHIPOTLE MAYO

serves 4

¾ teaspoon salt

¾ teaspoon dried oregano

½ teaspoon ground cumin

1 large yellow bell pepper, quartered

1 small red onion, cut into 4 thick slices

1 (1-pound) lean flank steak, trimmed

2 tablespoons light mayonnaise

1 tablespoon minced chipotles en adobo

1 tablespoon chopped fresh cilantro

4 light hamburger buns, toasted

1 beefsteak tomato, cut into 8 slices

1 Spray grill rack with nonstick spray. Preheat grill to medium-high or prepare medium-high fire.

2 Stir together salt, oregano, and cumin in small cup. Combine bell pepper and onion in medium bowl and spray lightly with nonstick spray. Sprinkle vegetables with half of seasoning mixture and toss to coat. Sprinkle steak with remaining seasoning.

3 Place vegetables and steak on grill rack and grill, turning occasionally, until vegetables are tender and instant-read thermometer inserted into side of steak registers 145°F, about 10 minutes. Transfer steak to cutting board and let stand 5 minutes.

4 Meanwhile, stir together mayonnaise, chipotles en adobo, and cilantro in small bowl.

5 Cut steak across grain into thin slices. Cut bell pepper into thin strips and separate onion into rings.

6 Spread mayonnaise mixture evenly on bottoms of buns. Top evenly with tomato slices, steak, bell pepper, and onion. Top with bun tops.

 6 SmartPoints value

Per serving (1 sandwich): 295 Cal, 10 g Total Fat, 3 g Sat Fat, 766 mg Sod, 24 g Total Carb, 5 g Sugar, 5 g Fib, 29 g Prot.

 *cook's tip*

Serve the sandwiches with sweet potatoes. Prick 4 small sweet potatoes with a fork. Microwave on High, rearranging once, until tender, about 10 minutes. One small sweet potato per serving will increase the SmartPoints value by 2.

SPICE-RUBBED MANGO-GLAZED PORK TENDERLOIN

serves 4 *gluten free*

⅓ cup mango chutney, large pieces chopped

1½ tablespoons dark rum

2 teaspoons cinnamon

1 teaspoon salt

½ teaspoon ground allspice

¼ teaspoon black pepper

1 (1-pound) lean pork tenderloin, trimmed

1 Spray grill rack with nonstick spray. Preheat grill to medium-high or prepare medium-high fire.

2 To make glaze, stir together chutney and rum in small cup and set aside.

3 Stir together cinnamon, salt, allspice, and pepper in another cup. Spread spice mixture all over tenderloin, and then lightly spray with nonstick spray. Place tenderloin on grill rack and grill, turning occasionally, 10 minutes.

4 Continue to grill pork, turning and brushing with glaze, until instant-read thermometer inserted into center registers 145°F, about 10 minutes longer. Transfer to cutting board and let rest 5 minutes. Cut into 12 slices.

5 SmartPoints value

Per serving (3 slices): 188 Cal, 4 g Total Fat, 1 g Sat Fat, 695 mg Sod, 10 g Total Carb, 8 g Sugar, 1 g Fib, 24 g Prot.

cook's tip

To make a side, spray slices of eggplant or zucchini with olive-oil nonstick spray. Grill, turning occasionally, until tender, about 8 minutes.

MOO SHU PORK STIR-FRY

serves 4

⅓ cup hoisin sauce

2 teaspoons Asian (dark) sesame oil

1 teaspoon minced garlic

1 teaspoon minced peeled fresh ginger

1 teaspoon rice vinegar

1 teaspoon sambal oelek

1 pound lean pork tenderloin, trimmed

1 teaspoon kosher salt

¼ teaspoon black pepper

½ pound fresh shiitake mushrooms, stems removed, caps sliced

1 (14-ounce) package coleslaw mix

6 scallions, chopped

3 tablespoons chopped fresh cilantro

1 Whisk together hoisin sauce, sesame oil, garlic, ginger, vinegar, and sambal oelek in small bowl. Set aside.

2 Cut pork into 4 pieces and cut each piece into thin strips. Sprinkle pork with salt and pepper.

3 Heat large wok or large deep skillet over medium-high heat until drop of water sizzles on it. Spray wok with nonstick spray. Add pork in three batches and stir-fry until browned, 3–4 minutes, spraying wok with nonstick spray between batches. Transfer pork to plate and keep warm.

4 Spray wok with nonstick spray. Add mushrooms and stir-fry until tender, about 5 minutes. Add coleslaw and hoisin sauce mixture and stir-fry until cabbage wilts, about 4 minutes.

5 Remove from heat and stir in pork, scallions, and cilantro.

 Per serving (1¼ cups): 253 Cal, 6 g Total Fat, 1 g Sat Fat, 921 mg Sod, 22 g Total Carb, 10 g Sugar, 5 g Fib, 28 g Prot.

 *cook's tip* — *Sambal oelek is an Asian chili sauce made with chiles and vinegar. If you can't find it, you can substitute Sriracha.*

GRILLED PORK WITH ARUGULA AND TOMATO SALAD

serves 4   *gluten free*   *under 20 minutes*

1¼ pounds lean pork tenderloin, trimmed and cut into 8 (¾-inch) slices

4 tablespoons lemon juice

2 garlic cloves, chopped

¾ teaspoon salt

½ teaspoon freshly ground black pepper

8 cups arugula

2 cups cherry tomatoes, halved

1 tablespoon extra-virgin olive oil

1 teaspoon balsamic vinegar

1 Place pork in large zip-close plastic bag. Add 2 tablespoons lemon juice, garlic, ½ teaspoon salt, and ¼ teaspoon pepper and turn to coat. Let stand 10 minutes.

2 Spray large ridged grill pan with nonstick spray and set over medium-high heat. Remove pork from marinade and discard marinade. Place pork in pan and cook, turning once, until instant-read thermometer inserted into sides of pork registers 145°F, about 6 minutes.

3 Meanwhile, to make salad, combine arugula, tomatoes, remaining 2 tablespoons lemon juice, oil, vinegar, remaining ¼ teaspoon salt, and remaining ¼ teaspoon pepper in large bowl. Toss to combine.

4 Divide pork among 4 plates and top evenly with salad.

 Per serving (2 slices pork and 2¼ cups salad): 217 Cal, 7 g Total Fat, 2 g Sat Fat, 526 mg Sod, 7 g Total Carb, 3 g Sugar, 2 g Fib, 32 g Prot.

Grilled Pork with Arugula and Tomato Salad

Pork Medallions with Indian-Spiced Squash Sauté

PORK MEDALLIONS WITH INDIAN-SPICED SQUASH SAUTÉ

serves 4   *gluten free*   *under 20 minutes*

1¼ pounds lean pork tenderloin, trimmed and cut into 8 (¾-inch) slices

¾ teaspoon salt

¼ teaspoon coarsely ground black pepper

3 teaspoons canola oil

1 garlic clove, chopped

2 small zucchini, thinly sliced

2 small yellow squash, thinly sliced

½ cup chopped red onion

½ teaspoon curry powder

½ teaspoon ground coriander

½ teaspoon ground cumin

1 Sprinkle pork with ½ teaspoon salt and pepper. Heat 2 teaspoons oil in large skillet over medium-high heat. Add pork in two batches and cook, turning once, until instant-read thermometer inserted into sides of pork registers 145°F, about 6 minutes. Transfer to platter and keep warm.

2 Reduce heat to medium and add remaining 1 teaspoon oil and garlic to skillet. Cook, stirring constantly, until garlic is fragrant, 30 seconds. Add zucchini, yellow squash, and onion. Cook, covered, stirring occasionally, until vegetables are crisp-tender, about 5 minutes. Stir in curry powder, coriander, cumin, and remaining ¼ teaspoon salt. Serve pork with vegetables.

 Per serving (2 slices pork and ¾ cup vegetables): 218 Cal, 7 g Total Fat, 1 g Sat Fat, 520 mg Sod, 7 g Total Carb, 4 g Sugar, 2 g Fib, 32 g Prot.

cook's tip

Cooking the pork in two batches adds a few minutes to the time to make this dish, but the beautifully browned and flavorful meat is worth the extra effort.

LEMON PORK AND SNAP PEA STIR-FRY

 serves 4 *gluten free*

- 1 (¾-pound) piece lean pork tenderloin, trimmed, quartered lengthwise, and cut into ¼-inch slices
- 2 tablespoons dry white wine
- 2 tablespoons canola oil
- 1 tablespoon minced garlic
- 2 teaspoons cornstarch
- 1 teaspoon salt
- 3 tablespoons reduced-sodium chicken broth
- ½ cup sliced red onion
- 2 cups sugar snap peas, trimmed
- ¼ teaspoon black pepper
- 2 tablespoons chopped fresh basil
- 1½ teaspoons grated lemon zest
- 3 tablespoons lemon juice

1 Combine pork, 1 tablespoon wine, 1 teaspoon oil, garlic, cornstarch, and ½ teaspoon salt in medium bowl and toss to coat. Set aside.

2 Stir together broth and remaining 1 tablespoon wine in small bowl. Set aside.

3 Heat large deep skillet or wok over medium-high heat until a drop of water sizzles on it. Add 1 tablespoon of remaining oil to skillet. Add onion and stir-fry 10 seconds. Push onion to side of pan. Add pork mixture to skillet, arranging pork in single layer. Cook without stirring 1 minute; then stir-fry until pork is no longer pink, about 1 minute longer.

4 Add remaining 2 teaspoons oil to skillet. Add sugar snap peas and stir-fry until bright green, about 30 seconds. Add reserved broth mixture, pepper, and remaining ½ teaspoon salt to skillet and stir-fry until pork is cooked through, 1–2 minutes. Remove from heat and stir in basil and lemon zest and juice.

 Per serving (1 cup): 195 Cal, 9 g Total Fat, 2 g Sat Fat, 712 mg Sod, 9 g Total Carb, 2 g Sugar, 2 g Fib, 19 g Prot.

 *cook's tip*

Serve this saucy dish with rice (½ cup cooked brown rice per serving will increase the SmartPoints value by 4).

PORK CHOPS WITH GINGER-LIME PEACH SALSA

serves 4 *gluten free* *under 20 minutes*

½ teaspoon plus pinch salt

2 teaspoons light brown sugar

1 teaspoon curry powder

1 teaspoon ground cumin

4 (¼-pound) lean boneless center-cut pork loin chops, trimmed

3 large peaches, peeled, halved, pitted, and chopped

1 scallion, thinly sliced

1 jalapeño pepper, seeded and minced

2 tablespoons chopped fresh cilantro

1 tablespoon lime juice

1 teaspoon grated peeled fresh ginger

1 Stir together ½ teaspoon salt, brown sugar, curry powder, and cumin in small cup. Rub pork chops with seasoning mixture.

2 Spray large ridged grill pan with nonstick spray and set over medium-high heat. Place pork in pan and cook, turning once, until instant-read thermometer inserted into sides of chops registers 145°F, about 6 minutes.

3 Meanwhile, to make salsa, combine peaches, scallion, jalapeño, cilantro, lime juice, ginger, and remaining pinch salt in medium bowl and toss to combine. Serve pork chops with salsa.

 Per serving (1 pork chop and ½ cup salsa): 231 Cal, 7 g Total Fat, 2 g Sat Fat, 422 mg Sod, 17 g Total Carb, 14 g Sugar, 3 g Fib, 24 g Prot.

cook's tip

Instead of peaches, you can use nectarines or mangoes for this salsa.

PORK CHOPS WITH FIG SAUCE AND PARMESAN GREEN BEANS

serves 4 • *gluten free*   • *under 20 minutes*

4 (¼-pound) lean boneless center-cut pork loin chops, trimmed

¾ teaspoon salt

½ teaspoon black pepper

2 teaspoons olive oil

¼ cup finely chopped onion

¼ cup reduced-sodium chicken broth

2 tablespoons fig jam

½ cup water

1 pound pretrimmed fresh green beans

2 tablespoons grated Parmesan

1 Sprinkle pork with ½ teaspoon salt and ¼ teaspoon pepper. Heat oil in medium skillet over medium-high heat. Add pork and cook, turning once, until instant-read thermometer inserted into sides of each chop registers 145°F, about 6 minutes. Transfer to plate and keep warm.

2 To make sauce, reduce heat to medium. Add onion to skillet and cook, stirring constantly, until onion is golden, about 1 minute. Add broth and jam to skillet. Cook, stirring to scrape up browned bits on bottom of skillet, until jam is melted, 1–2 minutes.

3 Meanwhile, bring water to boil in large skillet. Add green beans and cook, covered, just until crisp-tender, about 5 minutes. Drain and toss with Parmesan, remaining ¼ teaspoon salt, and remaining ¼ teaspoon pepper. Place green beans on serving platter. Top with chops and spoon sauce over chops.

 6 SmartPoints value

Per serving (1 pork chop, 1 tablespoon sauce, and 1 cup green beans): 261 Cal, 10 g Total Fat, 3 g Sat Fat, 576 mg Sod, 16 g Total Carb, 7 g Sugar, 4 g Fib, 26 g Prot.

 *cook's tip*

Fig jam gives this sauce a sweet, complex flavor. Look for it in large supermarkets and specialty food markets.

Pork Chops with Fig Sauce and Parmesan Green Beans

PORK CHOPS AND VEGETABLES WITH YELLOW CURRY SAUCE

serves 4 🍽 *gluten free* 🚫

4 (¼-pound) lean boneless center-cut pork loin chops, trimmed

½ teaspoon salt

⅛ teaspoon black pepper

2 teaspoons canola oil

1 red onion, chopped

1 green bell pepper, chopped

1 red bell pepper, chopped

1½ tablespoons Thai yellow curry paste

1 garlic clove, minced

1 teaspoon grated peeled fresh ginger

¾ pound cremini mushrooms, sliced

1 cup light (low-fat) coconut milk

¼ cup reduced-sodium chicken broth

2 teaspoons brown sugar

1 teaspoon lime juice

Chopped fresh cilantro

1 Sprinkle pork with salt and black pepper. Heat oil in large skillet over medium-high heat. Add pork and cook, turning once, until instant-read thermometer inserted into sides of chops registers 145°F, about 6 minutes. Transfer to plate and keep warm.

2 Add onion and bell peppers to skillet. Reduce heat to medium and cook, stirring often, until vegetables begin to soften, about 4 minutes. Add curry paste, garlic, and ginger and cook, stirring constantly, until fragrant, about 30 seconds. Stir in mushrooms, coconut milk, broth, and brown sugar and bring to simmer, scraping up browned bits from bottom of skillet. Cook, stirring occasionally, until mushrooms are tender, about 5 minutes. Remove from heat and stir in lime juice and any accumulated juices from chops.

3 Place pork chops on 4 plates and top evenly with vegetables and sauce. Sprinkle with cilantro.

 7 SmartPoints value

Per serving (1 pork chop and ¾ cup vegetables and sauce): 287 Cal, 13 g Total Fat, 4 g Sat Fat, 482 mg Sod, 16 g Total Carb, 8 g Sugar, 3 g Fib, 27 g Prot.

cook's tip

Thai yellow curry paste is the mildest variety, yet it is still quite spicy. If you're concerned about the heat, start with only 2 teaspoons of curry paste in this recipe.

PORK CHOPS WITH BRAISED CABBAGE AND RAISINS

serves 4   *gluten free*   *under 20 minutes*

- 2 teaspoons olive oil
- 4 (¼-pound) lean boneless center-cut pork loin chops, trimmed
- ½ teaspoon ground cumin
- ½ teaspoon salt
- 1 onion, thinly sliced
- 3 cups thinly sliced red cabbage
- ½ cup apple cider
- ¼ cup golden raisins, chopped
- ¾ teaspoon fennel seeds, lightly crushed
- ¼ teaspoon black pepper
- ½ teaspoon apple cider vinegar

1 Heat 1 teaspoon oil in large skillet over medium heat. Sprinkle chops with cumin and ¼ teaspoon salt. Add chops to skillet and cook, turning once, until instant-read thermometer inserted into sides of chops registers 145°F, about 6 minutes. Transfer to plate and keep warm.

2 Add remaining 1 teaspoon oil to skillet. Add onion and cook, stirring occasionally, until onion begins to soften, about 3 minutes. Add cabbage, cider, raisins, fennels seeds, and pepper and bring to boil. Reduce heat and simmer, stirring occasionally, until cabbage is crisp-tender, about 8 minutes. Stir in vinegar and remaining ¼ teaspoon salt. Serve chops with cabbage.

 Per serving (1 pork chop and ⅔ cup cabbage): 253 Cal, 9 g Total Fat, 2 g Sat Fat, 367 mg Sod, 19 g Total Carb, 12 g Sugar, 2 g Fib, 25 g Prot.

*Rosemary Lamb Chops
with Balsamic Tomatoes*

ROSEMARY LAMB CHOPS WITH BALSAMIC TOMATOES

serves 4   gluten free   under 20 minutes

2   teaspoons olive oil

4   (¼-pound) lean bone-in
    loin lamb chops, trimmed
    (1¼ inches thick)

2   tablespoons chopped
    fresh rosemary

¾   teaspoon salt

¼   teaspoon black pepper

2   cups cherry tomatoes

2   scallions, thinly sliced

2   tablespoons balsamic
    vinegar

1 Heat 1 teaspoon oil in large skillet over medium-high heat. Sprinkle lamb with rosemary, ½ teaspoon salt, and ⅛ teaspoon pepper. Place lamb in skillet and cook, turning once, until instant-read thermometer inserted into sides of chops registers 145°F, about 10 minutes. Transfer lamb to plate and keep warm.

2 Reduce heat to medium and add remaining 1 teaspoon oil to skillet. Add tomatoes and scallions and cook, stirring often, just until tomatoes are softened, about 2 minutes. Add vinegar, remaining ¼ teaspoon salt, and remaining ⅛ teaspoon pepper and cook 30 seconds. Serve lamb with tomatoes.

 Per serving (1 lamb chop and ½ cup tomatoes): 206 Cal, 9 g Total Fat, 3 g Sat Fat, 520 mg Sod, 5 g Total Carb, 3 g Sugar, 1 g Fib, 25 g Prot.

cook's tip

These simple yet flavorful balsamic tomatoes are also delicious served over salmon fillets or grilled chicken breasts.

chapter 3

CHEAP EATS:
GROUND TURKEY, GROUND BEEF, EGGS & BEANS

TERIYAKI TURKEY BURGERS

serves 4   **under 20 minutes** 🕐

1¼ pounds ground lean turkey

¼ cup teriyaki sauce

¼ cup chopped scallions

2 tablespoons chopped fresh cilantro

1 large egg white

1 tablespoon minced peeled fresh ginger

1 tablespoon minced garlic

1 teaspoon Asian (dark) sesame oil

8 scallions, trimmed and left whole

4 light hamburger buns, toasted

1 Mix turkey, teriyaki sauce, chopped scallions, cilantro, egg white, ginger, garlic, and sesame oil in medium bowl just until combined. With damp hands, form mixture into 4 (¾-inch-thick) patties.

2 Spray ridged grill pan with nonstick spray and set over medium heat. Add patties and whole scallions and cook, turning patties once and turning scallions occasionally, until instant-read thermometer inserted into side of patties registers 165°F and scallions are tender, about 10 minutes.

3 Serve burgers in buns topped with scallions.

 Per serving (1 burger): 331 Cal, 13 g Total Fat, 4 g Sat Fat, 997 mg Sod, 25 g Total Carb, 4 g Sugar, 4 g Fib, 34 g Prot.

cook's tip

The sweet and savory flavor of teriyaki sauce adds zip to these burgers. It also makes a delicious spread for the buns or as a dipping sauce for chilled shrimp. One tablespoon of teriyaki sauce has 1 SmartPoints value.

ASIAN TURKEY LETTUCE WRAPS

serves 4   *under 20 minutes*

1   teaspoon canola oil

3   scallions, thinly sliced

1   yellow or red bell pepper, diced

1   teaspoon grated peeled fresh ginger

1   pound ground lean turkey

3   tablespoons reduced-sodium soy sauce

½   teaspoon chili-garlic sauce

8   large iceberg or Bibb lettuce leaves

¼   cup chopped fresh cilantro

Lime wedges

1 Heat oil in large skillet over medium-high heat. Add scallions, bell pepper, and ginger and cook, stirring constantly, until vegetables just begin to soften, about 1 minute.

2 Add turkey and cook, breaking it apart with wooden spoon, until browned and cooked through, about 5 minutes. Stir in soy sauce and chili-garlic sauce.

3 Divide turkey mixture evenly among lettuce leaves. Sprinkle evenly with cilantro. Roll up tightly and serve at once with lime wedges.

 Per serving (2 wraps): 174 Cal, 6 g Total Fat, 1 g Sat Fat, 445 mg Sod, 3 g Total Carb, 1 g Sugar, 1 g Fib, 27 g Prot.

cook's tip

For extra spice, serve additional chili-garlic paste with the wraps.

TURKEY AND WHITE BEAN CHILI

serves 4   gluten free

2 teaspoons canola oil

1 pound ground lean turkey

½ teaspoon salt

1 red onion, chopped

1 large red or orange bell pepper, diced

1 garlic clove, crushed through garlic press

1½ teaspoons ground cumin

½ teaspoon dried oregano

¼ teaspoon cinnamon

⅛ teaspoon cayenne

1 (15½-ounce) can great northern beans, rinsed and drained

1 (12-ounce) jar salsa verde

1 cup reduced-sodium chicken broth

4 tablespoons plain fat-free Greek yogurt

Chopped fresh cilantro

Lime wedges

1 Heat oil in Dutch oven over medium-high heat. Add turkey and salt and cook, breaking turkey apart with wooden spoon, until no longer pink, 2–3 minutes.

2 Add onion and bell pepper. Cook, covered, stirring occasionally, until vegetables are tender, 3–4 minutes. Add garlic, cumin, oregano, cinnamon, and cayenne and cook, stirring constantly, until fragrant, 30 seconds. Stir in beans, salsa, and broth and bring to boil. Reduce heat to low and simmer, covered, 10 minutes.

3 Ladle chili into 4 bowls, top with yogurt, and sprinkle with cilantro. Serve with lime wedges.

 Per serving (1½ cups chili and 1 tablespoon yogurt): 377 Cal, 12 g Total Fat, 3 g Sat Fat, 927 mg Sod, 35 g Total Carb, 7 g Sugar, 8 g Fib, 34 g Prot.

double duty

Make a double batch of the chili and cover and refrigerate up to 4 days, or freeze up to 3 months.

Turkey and White Bean Chili

Thai Turkey, Noodle, and Asparagus Salad

THAI TURKEY, NOODLE, AND ASPARAGUS SALAD

serves 6   gluten free   under 20 minutes

¼ pound rice stick noodles, broken into 3-inch pieces

3 tablespoons rice vinegar

1 teaspoon grated lime zest

2 tablespoons lime juice

1 tablespoon dark brown sugar

1 tablespoon Asian fish sauce

1 tablespoon Asian (dark) sesame oil

2 teaspoons chili-garlic sauce

1 pound ground lean turkey

½ teaspoon five-spice powder

¼ teaspoon salt

½ pound asparagus, trimmed and cut into 1-inch pieces

3 garlic cloves, minced

1 tablespoon minced peeled fresh ginger

¼ cup chopped fresh cilantro plus leaves for sprinkling

3 tablespoons unsalted dry-roasted peanuts, coarsely chopped

1 Cook noodles according to package directions. Drain and rinse under cold running water. Drain again and transfer to large bowl.

2 Meanwhile, to make dressing, whisk together vinegar, lime zest and juice, brown sugar, fish sauce, sesame oil, and chili-garlic sauce in small bowl until brown sugar dissolves.

3 Spray large skillet with nonstick spray and set over medium-high heat. Add turkey, five-spice powder, and salt. Cook, breaking apart turkey with wooden spoon, until no longer pink and most of liquid has evaporated, about 5 minutes. Add turkey mixture to noodles.

4 Wipe out skillet with paper towel. Spray with nonstick spray and set over medium-high heat. Add asparagus, garlic, and ginger. Cook, stirring constantly, just until asparagus turns bright green, 1–2 minutes. Add asparagus mixture to noodle mixture. Add dressing and chopped cilantro and toss to combine. Sprinkle with peanuts and cilantro leaves. Serve at once.

 6 SmartPoints value

Per serving (1 cup): 246 Cal, 10 g Total Fat, 3 g Sat Fat, 425 mg Sod, 21 g Total Carb, 3 g Sugar, 2 g Fib, 18 g Prot.

cook's tip

Choose asparagus based on what looks freshest rather than by the size of the spears. Both thick and slender spears are tender and flavorful and cook in about the same time.

TURKEY PICADILLO TACOS

serves 4   *gluten free*

1 teaspoon olive oil

1 pound ground lean turkey

¼ teaspoon salt

1 small onion, chopped

1 celery stalk, halved lengthwise and sliced

1 large garlic clove, finely chopped

2 teaspoons ground cumin

½ teaspoon cinnamon

¼ teaspoon black pepper

1 cup jarred salsa

¼ cup raisins, coarsely chopped

¼ cup pimiento-stuffed olives, sliced

8 (6-inch) corn tortillas, warmed

2 cups thinly sliced iceberg lettuce

⅓ cup plain low-fat (1%) Greek yogurt

1 cup fresh cilantro sprigs

Lime wedges

1 Heat oil in large skillet and set over medium-high heat. Add turkey and salt and cook, breaking turkey apart with wooden spoon, until no longer pink, about 3 minutes.

2 Add onion and celery. Cook, covered, stirring occasionally, until vegetables are golden and tender, about 4 minutes. Add garlic, cumin, cinnamon, and pepper and cook, stirring constantly, until fragrant, 30 seconds.

3 Stir in salsa, raisins, and olives and cook, stirring occasionally, until heated through, about 3 minutes.

4 Fill each tortilla with scant ⅓ cup turkey mixture and ¼ cup lettuce. Top evenly with yogurt and cilantro sprigs. Serve with lime wedges.

 Per serving (2 tacos): 410 Cal, 16 g Total Fat, 4 g Sat Fat, 955 mg Sod, 38 g Total Carb, 10 g Sugar, 6 g Fib, 29 g Prot.

BEEF AND ZITI 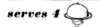 WITH ROASTED PEPPERS AND GREEN OLIVES

serves 4

6 ounces ziti

2 teaspoons olive oil

1 pound ground lean beef (7% fat or less)

¼ teaspoon black pepper

1 large red onion, chopped

2 garlic cloves, finely chopped

¾ teaspoon dried oregano

¼ teaspoon red pepper flakes

1 cup roasted red peppers (not oil-packed), drained and diced

16 green olives, drained (reserving 2 tablespoons brine) and coarsely chopped

¼ cup chopped fresh parsley

1 Cook ziti 2 minutes less than package directions specify. Drain, reserving ½ cup pasta cooking water.

2 Meanwhile, heat oil in large skillet over medium-high heat. Add beef and black pepper and cook, breaking beef apart with wooden spoon, until no longer pink, 4–5 minutes.

3 Add onion and cook, covered, stirring occasionally, until golden, about 5 minutes. Add garlic, oregano, and red pepper flakes and cook, stirring, until fragrant, about 30 seconds. Stir in roasted peppers, olives, and brine. Cook until heated through, 1–2 minutes.

4 Reduce heat to medium. Add pasta and reserved cooking water to skillet and cook, stirring often, until pasta is just tender, about 2 minutes. Remove from heat and stir in parsley.

 Per serving (1½ cups) 400 Cal, 10 g Total Fat, 3 g Sat Fat, 424 mg Sod, 46 g Total Carb, 6 g Sugar, 3 g Fib, 31 g Prot.

 *cook's tip*

If you have fresh basil on hand, use it instead of the parsley for even more flavor in this dish.

TURKEY TACO SALAD

serves 4   *under 20 minutes*

2 teaspoons canola oil

1 pound ground lean turkey

1 teaspoon ancho chile powder

½ teaspoon ground cumin

¼ teaspoon salt

1 cup jarred green salsa

1 large head romaine lettuce, separated into leaves

12 baked tortilla chips, broken into large pieces

½ cup shredded reduced-fat Mexican cheese blend

1 avocado, halved, pitted, peeled, and sliced

1 cup grape tomatoes, halved

½ small English (seedless) cucumber, sliced

¼ cup light sour cream

Lime wedges

1 Heat oil in large skillet over medium-high heat. Add turkey and cook, breaking it apart with wooden spoon, until no longer pink, about 3 minutes. Stir in chile powder, cumin, and salt and cook, stirring, 1 minute. Stir in ½ cup salsa and cook until heated through, 1–2 minutes.

2 Divide lettuce among 4 plates. Top evenly with turkey mixture, tortilla chips, cheese, avocado, tomatoes, cucumber, and sour cream. Drizzle salads with remaining ½ cup salsa and serve with lime wedges.

10 SmartPoints value **Per serving** (1 salad): 417 Cal, 25 g Total Fat, 7 g Sat Fat, 767 mg Sod, 23 g Total Carb, 5 g Sugar, 8 g Fib, 31 g Prot.

cook's tip

If you prefer tomato salsa, you can use it in this recipe instead of the green salsa.

*Turkey
Taco Salad*

SPICED BEEF RAGU

serves 6

½ pound whole wheat fusilli

¾ pound ground lean beef (7% fat or less)

¾ teaspoon salt

¼ teaspoon black pepper

2 carrots, finely chopped

1 small onion, finely chopped

1 small fennel bulb, cored and finely chopped

1 teaspoon ground cumin

1 teaspoon ground coriander

¼ teaspoon red pepper flakes

1½ pounds tomatoes, cut into ¾-inch pieces

6 tablespoons crumbled feta

½ cup chopped fresh mint

1 Cook pasta according to package directions. Transfer to large bowl and keep warm.

2 Meanwhile, spray large skillet with olive-oil nonstick spray and set over medium-high heat. Add beef, ½ teaspoon salt, and black pepper and cook, breaking beef apart with wooden spoon, until no longer pink, 4–5 minutes.

3 Stir in carrots, onion, and fennel. Cook, covered, stirring occasionally, until vegetables are tender, about 5 minutes. Add cumin, coriander, and red pepper flakes and cook, stirring constantly, until fragrant, 30 seconds.

4 Stir in tomatoes and remaining ¼ teaspoon salt and bring to boil. Reduce heat to low and simmer, covered, stirring occasionally, until tomatoes are softened, about 5 minutes.

5 Add beef mixture to pasta and toss to combine. Divide evenly among 6 bowls. Sprinkle evenly with feta and mint.

6 SmartPoints value

Per serving (1⅓ cups): 282 Cal, 6 g Total Fat, 3 g Sat Fat, 479 mg Sod, 40 g Total Carb, 5 g Sugar, 8 g Fib, 21 g Prot.

cook's tip

If fresh tomatoes are not at their peak, substitute a 28-ounce can of diced tomatoes in this recipe and simmer the sauce, uncovered, until it thickens slightly, about 10 minutes.

QUICK BEEF AND PINTO BEAN CHILI

serves 4 *gluten free* *under 20 minutes*

- 1 pound ground lean beef (7% fat or less)
- 1 garlic clove, minced
- 2 teaspoons chili powder
- ½ teaspoon salt
- ¼ teaspoon dried oregano
- ¼ teaspoon black pepper
- 1 (15½-ounce) can pinto beans, rinsed and drained
- 1 (14½-ounce) can diced tomatoes with chipotle chiles
- 1 cup canned fire-roasted crushed tomatoes
- 1 (8-ounce) package frozen chopped green peppers and onions

1 Spray large saucepan with nonstick spray and set over medium-high heat. Add beef, garlic, chili powder, salt, oregano, and black pepper and cook, breaking beef apart with wooden spoon until browned, 5–7 minutes.

2 Add beans, diced tomatoes, crushed tomatoes, and peppers and onions and bring to boil. Reduce heat and simmer, stirring often, until chili thickens slightly, about 3 minutes.

6 SmartPoints value

Per serving (1¼ cups): 286 Cal, 7 g Total Fat, 3 g Sat Fat, 894 mg Sod, 26 g Total Carb, 5 g Sugar, 8 g Fib, 31 g Prot.

cook's tip

Top the chili with 0 SmartPoints toppings such as sliced scallions, diced fresh tomatoes, minced jalapeño, or chopped fresh cilantro.

Beef and
Portobello Burgers

BEEF AND PORTOBELLO BURGERS

serves 4   *under 20 minutes*

6 ounces portobello mushroom caps

¾ pound ground lean beef (7% fat or less)

2 tablespoons dried whole wheat bread crumbs

½ teaspoon salt

¼ teaspoon black pepper

1 teaspoon canola oil

¼ cup light mayonnaise

2 tablespoons chopped fresh basil

1 garlic clove, minced

4 light hamburger buns, split

4 thick tomato slices

4 green leaf lettuce leaves

1 Place mushrooms in food processor and pulse until minced. Transfer mushrooms to large bowl. Add beef, bread crumbs, salt, and pepper and stir to combine. With damp hands, shape mixture into 4 (½-inch-thick) patties.

2 Heat oil in large skillet over medium-high heat. Add patties and cook, turning once, until instant-read thermometer inserted into side of burgers registers 160°F, about 10 minutes.

3 Meanwhile, stir together mayonnaise, basil, and garlic in small bowl.

4 Spread mayonnaise mixture evenly on tops of buns. Serve burgers in buns and top evenly with tomato slices and lettuce leaves.

 7 SmartPoints value

Per serving (1 garnished burger): 287 Cal, 11 g Total Fat, 3 g Sat Fat, 640 mg Sod, 25 g Total Carb, 5 g Sugar, 4 g Fib, 24 g Prot.

cook's tip

The minced mushrooms in these burgers add flavor and keep the lean beef moist as it cooks.

GINGERY BEEF AND MUSHROOM LETTUCE WRAPS

serves 4   *under 20 minutes*

- 1 pound ground lean beef (7% fat or less)
- 1 cup thinly sliced onion
- 2 tablespoons minced peeled fresh ginger
- 2 garlic cloves, minced
- 2 cups thinly sliced bok choy
- 2 cups thinly sliced white mushrooms
- 1 red bell pepper, thinly sliced
- 3 tablespoons reduced-sodium soy sauce
- 8 large Bibb or leaf lettuce leaves
- ¼ cup thinly sliced fresh mint

Lime wedges

1 Spray large skillet with nonstick spray and set over medium-high heat. Add beef, onion, ginger, and garlic and cook, breaking beef apart with wooden spoon until browned, 5–7 minutes.

2 Add bok choy, mushrooms, bell pepper, and soy sauce and cook, stirring occasionally, until bok choy is wilted and bell pepper is crisp-tender, about 3 minutes.

3 Spoon about ½ cup beef mixture into each lettuce leaf. Sprinkle with mint and serve with lime wedges.

 Per serving (2 filled lettuce leaves): 204 Cal, 6 g Total Fat, 3 g Sat Fat, 504 mg Sod, 10 g Total Carb, 4 g Sugar, 3 g Fib, 28 g Prot.

 *cook's tip*

Instead of mint, you can top the wraps with fresh basil or cilantro.

Gingery Beef and Mushroom Lettuce Wraps

CANNELLINI BEANS WITH KALE AND BACON

 serves 4 *gluten free*

2 slices bacon

3 garlic cloves, minced

½ teaspoon red pepper flakes

1 onion, diced

1 pound kale, tough stems removed, leaves chopped

1 cup reduced-sodium chicken broth

1 (15½-ounce) can cannellini (white kidney) beans, rinsed and drained

1 tablespoon balsamic vinegar

1 teaspoon kosher salt

1 teaspoon raw (turbinado) sugar

1 Cook bacon in large skillet over medium-high heat until crisp. Transfer bacon to paper towel–lined plate to drain.

2 Add garlic and red pepper flakes to skillet and cook, stirring constantly, until fragrant, 30 seconds. Add onion and cook, stirring occasionally, until softened, about 3 minutes. Add kale and cook, stirring occasionally, until wilted, about 3 minutes.

3 Add broth and bring to boil. Reduce heat to low and simmer, covered, until kale is tender, about 5 minutes. Stir in beans and simmer, uncovered, until liquid is almost evaporated, about 3 minutes. Stir in vinegar, salt, and sugar.

4 Divide evenly among 4 shallow bowls. Crumble bacon evenly over each serving.

 Per serving (1¼ cups): 270 Cal, 8 g Total Fat, 2 g Sat Fat, 753 mg Sod, 39 g Total Carb, 3 g Sugar, 8 g Fib, 13 g Prot.

EGGS WITH POLENTA AND SPICY BLACK BEANS

 serves 6 gluten free vegetarian

1 (16-ounce) tube prepared polenta, cut into 12 (½-inch) slices

1 (15½-ounce) can black beans, rinsed and drained

1 cup fat-free salsa

½ teaspoon chili powder

2 teaspoons canola oil

6 large eggs

⅓ cup shredded reduced-fat pepper Jack

¼ cup chopped fresh cilantro

1 Preheat oven to 425°F. Spray baking sheet with nonstick spray.

2 Arrange polenta slices in single layer on prepared baking sheet. Spray polenta lightly with nonstick spray. Bake until hot, about 20 minutes.

3 Meanwhile, combine beans, salsa, and chili powder in small saucepan and bring to boil. Reduce heat and simmer, covered, about 10 minutes.

4 Heat oil in large nonstick over medium heat. Crack eggs into skillet and cook until yolks just begin to set, 2–3 minutes. Remove skillet from heat and sprinkle eggs with pepper Jack. Cover skillet and let stand until cheese melts, about 2 minutes.

5 Place 2 polenta slices on each of 6 plates. Spoon bean mixture evenly over polenta and top each with 1 egg. Sprinkle with cilantro and serve at once.

6 SmartPoints value

Per serving (2 slices polenta, ⅓ cup bean mixture, and 1 egg): 223 Cal, 7 g Total Fat, 3 g Sat Fat, 616 mg Sod, 26 g Total Carb, 2 g Sugar, 7 g Fib, 15 g Prot.

*Huevos
Mexicanos*

HUEVOS MEXICANOS

serves 4 　gluten free 🚫　vegetarian 🍃　under 20 minutes ⏱

4 plum tomatoes, chopped

1 small onion, diced

1 jalapeño pepper, seeded and thinly sliced

2 tablespoons chopped fresh cilantro

1 tablespoon lime juice

½ teaspoon salt

2 teaspoons distilled white vinegar

4 large eggs

4 (6-inch) fat-free corn tortillas, warmed

4 tablespoons shredded reduced-fat pepperJack

Lime wedges

1 To make salsa, stir together tomatoes, onion, jalapeño, cilantro, lime juice, and salt in medium bowl. Set aside.

2 Fill large skillet halfway with water and bring to boil over high heat. Add vinegar and reduce heat so water simmers slowly. Crack eggs and slip in, one at time, waiting about 10 seconds before adding another egg. Poach just until set, 3–5 minutes. Using slotted spoon, transfer eggs to paper towel-lined plate to drain.

3 Place 1 tortilla on each of 4 plates and top each with 1 tablespoon pepper Jack. Top each with 1 egg; top evenly with salsa. Serve at once with lime wedges.

 Per serving (1 filled tortilla): 180 Cal, 7 g Total Fat, 2 g Sat Fat, 527 mg Sod, 20 g Total Carb, 5 g Sugar, 3 g Fib, 11 g Prot.

MOZZARELLA, ROASTED PEPPER, AND BASIL OMELETTE

 serves 2 *gluten free* *vegetarian* *under 20 minutes*

2 large eggs

2 large egg whites

1 tablespoon fat-free milk

¼ teaspoon black pepper

⅛ teaspoon salt

1 teaspoon olive oil

⅓ cup shredded reduced-fat mozzarella

¼ cup roasted red peppers (not oil-packed), drained and thinly sliced

1 tablespoon thinly sliced fresh basil

1 Beat eggs, egg whites, milk, black pepper, and salt in medium bowl until frothy.

2 Heat oil in medium nonstick skillet over medium heat. Pour in egg mixture and cook, stirring gently, until eggs are almost set, about 2 minutes.

3 Sprinkle mozzarella, roasted peppers, and basil evenly over half of omelette. With spatula, fold other half over filling and continue to cook until filling is heated through and eggs are set, about 1 minute longer.

4 Cut omelette in half and slide each half onto 1 plate.

3 **SmartPoints value** **Per serving** (½ omelette): 154 Cal, 7 g Total Fat, 2 g Sat Fat, 502 mg Sod, 7 g Total Carb, 2 g Sugar, 0 g Fib, 16 g Prot.

Mozzarella, Roasted Pepper, and Basil Omelette

Pasta Soup with
Cannellini and Escarole

PASTA SOUP WITH CANNELLINI AND ESCAROLE

serves 4 🍲 *vegetarian* 🌿 *under 20 minutes* ⏱

½ cup ditalini pasta

2 teaspoons olive oil

2 garlic cloves, minced

4 cups packed chopped escarole

6 cups reduced-sodium vegetable broth

½ teaspoon dried oregano

¼ teaspoon salt

¼ teaspoon red pepper flakes

1 (15½-ounce) can cannellini (white kidney) beans, rinsed and drained

2 teaspoons lemon juice

4 tablespoons grated pecorino Romano

1 Cook ditalini according to package directions.

2 Meanwhile, heat oil in large saucepan over medium-high heat. Add garlic and cook, stirring constantly, until fragrant, 30 seconds. Add escarole and cook, stirring often, until wilted, about 1 minute. Add broth, oregano, salt, and red pepper flakes. Cover and bring to boil. Cook until escarole is tender, about 3 minutes.

3 Add beans and cook until heated through, about 2 minutes. Stir in ditalini. Remove from heat and stir in lemon juice.

4 Ladle soup evenly into 4 bowls and sprinkle evenly with pecorino.

 7 SmartPoints value

Per serving (about 2 cups soup and 1 tablespoon cheese): 252 Cal, 5 g Total Fat, 1 g Sat Fat, 571 mg Sod, 41 g Total Carb, 4 g Sugar, 7 g Fib, 12 g Prot.

 **cook's tip**

Instead of escarole, you can use chopped fresh kale, collards, or cabbage in this soup.

MEXICAN BLACK BEAN SOUP

serves 4   gluten free   vegetarian   under 20 minutes

1 teaspoon olive oil

1 onion, chopped

1 bell pepper, chopped

2 garlic cloves, minced

2 teaspoons ancho chile powder

1½ teaspoons ground cumin

1 (14½-ounce) can reduced-sodium vegetable broth

1 cup frozen corn kernels

2 (15½-ounce) cans black beans, rinsed and drained

¼ cup water

4 teaspoons lime juice

½ cup shredded reduced-fat Mexican cheese blend

1 Heat oil in large saucepan over medium-high heat. Add onion and bell pepper and cook, stirring occasionally, until softened, about 5 minutes. Stir in garlic, chile powder, and cumin and cook, stirring constantly, 30 seconds. Add broth, corn, and 1 can beans. Bring to simmer and cook 5 minutes.

2 Puree remaining can beans with water in blender. Stir pureed beans into soup, bring to simmer, and cook 2 minutes. Remove from heat and stir in lime juice. Ladle evenly into 4 bowls and sprinkle evenly with cheese.

8 SmartPoints value

Per serving (1½ cups soup and 2 tablespoons cheese): 320 Cal, 6 g Total Fat, 2 g Sat Fat, 1,170 mg Sod, 51 g Total Carb, 3 g Sugar, 18 g Fib, 20 g Prot.

double duty

Make a double batch of the soup and cover and refrigerate up to 4 days or freeze up to 3 months.

WHITE BEAN AND ALMOND BURGERS

serves 4   *under 20 minutes*   *vegetarian*

1   shallot

1   (15½-ounce) can cannellini (white kidney) beans, rinsed and drained

¼   cup plain dried bread crumbs

¼   cup chopped fresh cilantro

1   large egg

2   tablespoons slivered almonds

¾   teaspoon smoked paprika

¾   teaspoon ground coriander

¾   teaspoon ground cumin

½   teaspoon salt

½   teaspoon black pepper

2   teaspoons olive oil

2   tablespoons light mayonnaise

4   reduced-calorie hamburger buns, split and toasted

4   thin slices red onion

4   thick tomato slices

4   green leaf lettuce leaves

1 Place shallot in food processor and pulse until finely chopped. Add beans, bread crumbs, cilantro, egg, almonds, ½ teaspoon paprika, ½ teaspoon coriander, ½ teaspoon cumin, salt, and pepper. Pulse until mixture is well mashed.

2 Heat oil in large nonstick skillet over medium heat. Scoop bean mixture by ½ cup measures into skillet and flatten with spatula. Cook, turning once, until browned, about 8 minutes.

3 Meanwhile, stir together mayonnaise, remaining ¼ teaspoon paprika, ¼ teaspoon coriander, and ¼ teaspoon cumin in small bowl.

4 Serve burgers in buns with mayonnaise mixture, onion, tomato, and lettuce.

 9 SmartPoints value

Per serving (1 burger): 346 Cal, 10 g Total Fat, 2 g Sat Fat, 598 mg Sod, 54 g Total Carb, 6 g Sugar, 11 g Fib, 16 g Prot.

*Falafel Sandwiches
with Avocado Lime Sauce*

FALAFEL SANDWICHES WITH AVOCADO LIME SAUCE

 serves 4 vegetarian 🍃 under 20 minutes

½ small avocado, pitted and peeled

2 tablespoons light sour cream

2 tablespoons chopped tomato

1 tablespoon minced red onion

1 teaspoon lime juice

½ teaspoon salt

1 (15½-ounce) can pinto beans, rinsed and drained

½ cup shredded reduced-fat pepper Jack

¼ cup plain dried bread crumbs

2 scallions, thinly sliced

2 tablespoons chopped fresh cilantro

1 large egg, lightly beaten

¼ teaspoon ground cumin

2 teaspoons canola oil

1 cup thinly sliced romaine lettuce

2 (7-inch) pita breads, halved

Lime wedges

1 To make sauce, mash avocado in small bowl. Add sour cream, tomato, onion, lime juice, and salt and stir to combine.

2 Place beans in large bowl and coarsely mash with fork or potato masher. Add pepper Jack, bread crumbs, scallions, cilantro, egg, and cumin and stir to mix well. With damp hands, form mixture into 8 small patties.

3 Heat oil in large nonstick skillet over medium heat. Add patties and cook, turning once, until browned and crispy, about 6 minutes.

4 Divide lettuce evenly among pita halves. Place 2 falafel patties in each pita half and top evenly with sauce. Serve with lime wedges.

 Per serving (½ stuffed pita): 275 Cal, 10 g Total Fat, 3 g Sat Fat, 818 mg Sod, 33 g Total Carb, 3 g Sugar, 8 g Fib, 14 g Prot.

chapter 4

GREAT CATCH:
SEAFOOD

SALMON WITH COCONUT-TOMATO SAUCE

serves 4 · **gluten free** · **under 20 minutes**

2 teaspoons canola oil

1 small onion, finely chopped

1 tablespoon minced peeled fresh ginger

1 garlic clove, minced

½ cup canned petite-diced tomatoes

½ cup light (low-fat) coconut milk

Pinch cayenne

12 cherry tomatoes, halved

1 pound salmon fillets, cut into 1-inch pieces

½ teaspoon salt

3 tablespoons chopped fresh cilantro

2 teaspoons lime juice

1 Heat oil in large skillet over medium-high heat. Add onion and cook, stirring often, until softened, about 5 minutes. Add ginger and garlic and cook, stirring constantly, until fragrant, 30 seconds. Add diced tomatoes, coconut milk, and cayenne. Bring to boil. Reduce heat to low and simmer, covered, 5 minutes.

2 Add cherry tomatoes to skillet and simmer, covered, just until tomatoes begin to soften, 1–2 minutes. Sprinkle salmon with salt. Add salmon, cover, and simmer, stirring occasionally, until salmon is just opaque in center, 3–4 minutes. Remove skillet from heat and stir in cilantro and lime juice.

4 SmartPoints value · **Per serving** (1 cup): 208 Cal, 9 g Total Fat, 2 g Sat Fat, 427 mg Sod, 7 g Total Carb, 3 g Sugar, 1 g Fib, 25 g Prot.

cook's tip

To soak up the creamy coconut-tomato sauce, serve the salmon with rice (½ cup cooked brown rice will increase the SmartPoints value by 4).

*Salmon with
Coconut-Tomato Sauce*

Salmon with
Thai Slaw

SALMON WITH THAI SLAW

4 (6-ounce) skin-on salmon fillets

½ teaspoon salt

1 teaspoon grated lime zest

1 tablespoon lime juice

1 tablespoon Asian fish sauce

1 teaspoon sugar

1 teaspoon Asian (dark) sesame oil

½ small head Savoy cabbage, thinly sliced

½ cup shredded carrot

⅓ cup fresh cilantro leaves

⅓ cup fresh mint leaves

1 jalapeño pepper or small red Thai chile, seeded and minced

Lime wedges

1 Sprinkle salmon with salt. Spray large skillet with nonstick spray and set over medium-high heat. Add salmon, skin side down, and cook 4 minutes. Turn and cook until lightly browned and just opaque in center, about 4 minutes longer.

2 Meanwhile, to make slaw, whisk together lime zest and juice, fish sauce, sugar, and sesame oil in large bowl. Add cabbage, carrot, cilantro, mint, and jalapeño and toss to coat well.

3 Remove and discard skin from salmon. Serve salmon with slaw and lime wedges.

8 SmartPoints value

Per serving (1 salmon fillet and 1 cup slaw): 366 Cal, 20 g Total Fat, 4 g Sat Fat, 782 mg Sod, 11 g Total Carb, 5 g Sugar, 5 g Fib, 36 g Prot.

cook's tip

Savoy cabbage looks like a deeply wrinkled version of regular green cabbage. You can use green cabbage or Napa cabbage in this recipe if you prefer.

HONEY-MUSTARD ROASTED SALMON

serves 4   *gluten free*

4 (6-ounce) skinless wild pink salmon fillets, thawed if frozen

⅛ teaspoon salt

⅛ teaspoon coarsely ground black pepper

¼ cup Dijon mustard

4 teaspoons honey

1 tablespoon water

1 tablespoon white-wine vinegar

1 small garlic clove, crushed through garlic press

¼ teaspoon dry mustard

2 teaspoons chopped fresh dill

1 Preheat oven to 400°F. Spray large shallow baking dish with nonstick spray.

2 Sprinkle salmon with salt and pepper and place in prepared baking dish.

3 Whisk together Dijon, honey, water, vinegar, garlic, and dry mustard in small bowl. Remove 2 tablespoons mustard mixture and brush over salmon fillets. Stir dill into remaining mustard mixture and set aside.

4 Bake salmon until just opaque in center, about 15 minutes. Serve salmon with reserved mustard mixture.

 Per serving (1 fillet and 1½ tablespoons sauce): 253 Cal, 8 g Total Fat, 1 g Sat Fat, 544 mg Sod, 6 g Total Carb, 6 g Sugar, 0 g Fib, 35 g Prot.

cook's tip

Skinless wild pink salmon fillets are readily available in the frozen food department of most supermarkets.

GRILLED TUNA WITH FENNEL, ORANGE, AND OLIVE SALAD

serves 4 *gluten free*

- 4 (5-ounce) tuna steaks, ¾ inch thick
- ¾ teaspoon salt
- ¼ teaspoon black pepper
- 3 teaspoons olive oil
- 3 large navel oranges
- 2 scallions, thinly sliced
- 1 large fennel bulb, cored and very thinly sliced
- 12 pitted Kalamata olives, coarsely chopped
- 1 tablespoon red-wine vinegar
- 1 tablespoon chopped fresh fennel fronds or parsley

1 Sprinkle tuna with ½ teaspoon salt and ⅛ teaspoon pepper. Heat 1 teaspoon oil in large ridged grill pan over medium-high heat. Add tuna and cook, turning once, until browned on outside but still pink in center, about 5 minutes.

2 Meanwhile, to make salad, cut slice off top and bottom end of each orange. Stand orange on one end and slice off peel and white pith, turning orange as you cut. Cut orange in half lengthwise, then slice into half-moons. Place oranges in large bowl.

3 Add scallions, fennel, olives, vinegar, fennel fronds, remaining 2 teaspoons oil, remaining ¼ teaspoon salt, and remaining ⅛ teaspoon pepper to bowl and toss gently to combine. Serve tuna with salad.

3 SmartPoints value

Per serving (1 tuna steak and about 1 cup salad): 290 Cal, 6 g Total Fat, 1 g Sat Fat, 614 mg Sod, 23 g Total Carb, 13 g Sugar, 6 g Fib, 36 g Prot.

double duty

Grill extra tuna steaks to use for salads or sandwiches later in the week. Cooked tuna will stay fresh in the refrigerator up to 3 days.

PEPPERED TUNA WITH LEMONGRASS VINAIGRETTE

serves 4 *under 20 minutes*

¼ cup chopped fresh cilantro

2 tablespoons lime juice

2 tablespoons seasoned rice vinegar

1 tablespoon minced lemongrass

2 teaspoons reduced-sodium soy sauce

2 teaspoons olive oil

1 garlic clove, minced

4 (5-ounce) tuna steaks, ¾ inch thick

2 teaspoons cracked black pepper

½ teaspoon salt

4 cups mixed baby greens

1 Hass avocado, pitted, peeled, and cut into ½-inch pieces

1 To make vinaigrette, stir together cilantro, lime juice, vinegar, lemongrass, soy sauce, oil, and garlic in small bowl.

2 Spray large skillet with nonstick spray and set over medium-high heat. Sprinkle tuna with pepper and salt. Place in skillet and cook, turning once, until browned on outside but still pink in center, about 5 minutes.

3 Transfer tuna to cutting board and let stand 5 minutes. Cut tuna into ¼-inch-thick slices. Divide baby greens and avocado evenly among 4 plates. Top evenly with tuna and drizzle with vinaigrette.

 Per serving (1 plate): 261 Cal, 9 g Total Fat, 1 g Sat Fat, 481 mg Sod, 8 g Total Carb, 1 g Sugar, 5 g Fib, 37 g Prot.

 *cook's tip*

If lemongrass is not available, add a teaspoon of grated lime zest to the vinaigrette. The flavor won't be quite the same, but it will still be delicious.

*Peppered Tuna with
Lemongrass Vinaigrette*

Sautéed Halibut with Coconut Rice and Mango Salsa

SAUTÉED HALIBUT WITH COCONUT RICE AND MANGO SALSA

serves 4 *gluten free*

¾ cup chicken broth

½ cup light (low-fat) coconut milk

⅔ cup jasmine or basmati rice

¾ teaspoon salt

1 teaspoon olive oil

4 (5-ounce) skinless halibut fillets

¼ teaspoon freshly ground black pepper

1 mango, peeled, pitted, and diced

1 small red bell pepper, diced

2 tablespoons chopped fresh cilantro

1 tablespoon lime juice

1 teaspoon minced chipotle en adobo

1 Combine broth and coconut milk in medium saucepan. Set over medium-high heat and bring to boil. Stir in rice and ¼ teaspoon salt. Reduce heat to low and simmer, covered, until rice is tender and liquid is absorbed, about 18 minutes.

2 Meanwhile, heat oil in large skillet over medium-high heat. Sprinkle fish with ¼ teaspoon salt and black pepper. Add fish to skillet and cook, turning once, until just opaque in center, about 9 minutes.

3 Stir together mango, bell pepper, cilantro, lime juice, chipotle, and remaining ¼ teaspoon salt in small bowl.

4 Divide rice evenly among 4 plates. Top rice with fish fillets and spoon salsa evenly over fish.

 6 SmartPoints value

Per serving (1 fillet, ½ cup rice, and ½ cup salsa): 341 Cal, 6 g Total Fat, 2 g Sat Fat, 715 mg Sod, 42 g Total Carb, 14 g Sugar, 3 g Fib, 30 g Prot.

cook's tip

If you're in a hurry, skip making the fresh mango salsa and serve the fish with a purchased salsa.

FLOUNDER WITH BASIL-MINT TOMATOES

serves 4   *gluten free*  *under 20 minutes*

2 teaspoons olive oil

4 (6-ounce) skinless flounder fillets

¾ teaspoon salt

½ teaspoon black pepper

2 tomatoes, chopped

¼ cup thinly sliced fresh mint

¼ cup thinly sliced fresh basil

1 Heat oil in large nonstick skillet over medium heat. Sprinkle fish with ¼ teaspoon salt and ¼ teaspoon pepper. Add fish to skillet and cook, turning once, until just opaque in center, about 6 minutes. Transfer to serving platter and keep warm.

2 Meanwhile, stir together tomatoes, mint, basil, remaining ½ teaspoon salt, and remaining ¼ teaspoon pepper in medium bowl.

3 Add tomato mixture to skillet and cook, scraping up browned bits from bottom of pan, until heated through, about 2 minutes. Spoon tomato mixture over fish.

 Per serving (1 fillet and ½ cup tomatoes): 192 Cal, 5 g Total Fat, 1 g Sat Fat, 578 mg Sod, 4 g Total Carb, 2 g Sugar, 2 g Fib, 33 g Prot.

cook's tip

Instead of flounder, you can use any mild fish fillets in this recipe. Halibut, cod, and striped bass are good choices.

CRISPY JALAPEÑO-LIME FISH CAKES

serves 6

- 1 pound skinless cod fillets, coarsely chopped
- 1 small onion, grated and squeezed dry
- 1 large garlic clove, crushed through garlic press
- 1 small jalapeño pepper, seeded and minced
- ¼ cup chopped fresh cilantro
- 1 tablespoon lime juice
- ¾ teaspoon salt
- ½ cup plus 2 tablespoons plain dried bread crumbs
- 1 large egg, lightly beaten
- 2 teaspoons canola oil

Lime wedges

1 Stir together cod, onion, garlic, jalapeño, cilantro, lime juice, and salt in large bowl. Add ½ cup bread crumbs and egg, stirring until well mixed.

2 With damp hands, shape cod mixture into 6 (½-inch-thick) cakes. Sprinkle patties on both sides with remaining 2 tablespoons bread crumbs.

3 Heat oil in large nonstick skillet over medium heat. Add cakes to skillet and cook, turning once, until crispy, about 6 minutes. Serve with lime wedges.

3 SmartPoints value

Per serving (1 fish cake): 139 Cal, 3 g Total Fat, 1 g Sat Fat, 426 mg Sod, 10 g Total Carb, 1 g Sugar, 1 g Fib, 16 g Prot.

cook's tip

Serve the fish cakes with purchased fat-free salsa for 0 additional SmartPoints.

CATFISH AND VEGETABLE STIR-FRY

serves 4

1 pound catfish or tilapia fillets, cut into 1-inch pieces

1 tablespoon rice vinegar

2 teaspoons canola oil

3 garlic cloves, minced

1 tablespoon minced peeled fresh ginger

¼ teaspoon red pepper flakes

½ small head Savoy cabbage, thinly sliced

3 cups broccoli florets

2 carrots, thinly sliced diagonally

1 red bell pepper, thinly sliced

¾ cup reduced-sodium chicken broth

3 tablespoons reduced-sodium soy sauce

3 scallions, thinly sliced

2 tablespoons chopped fresh cilantro

1 Place catfish and vinegar in medium bowl and toss to coat. Set aside.

2 Set large wok or skillet over medium-high heat until drop of water sizzles in pan. Add oil and swirl to coat pan. Add garlic, ginger, and red pepper flakes and cook, stirring constantly, until fragrant, 10 seconds. Add cabbage, broccoli, carrots, and bell pepper and stir-fry until vegetables begin to soften, 4 minutes.

3 Add broth and soy sauce and bring to boil. Add catfish, cover, and cook, stirring occasionally, until catfish is just opaque throughout, 3 minutes. Remove from heat and stir in scallions.

4 Divide evenly among 4 plates and sprinkle with cilantro.

4 SmartPoints value — **Per serving** (2¼ cups): 262 Cal, 12 g Total Fat, 2 g Sat Fat, 596 mg Sod, 18 g Total Carb, 6 g Sugar, 7 g Fib, 24 g Prot.

*Catfish and
Vegetable Stir-Fry*

*Soy-Glazed Fish with
Stir-Fried Spinach*

SOY-GLAZED FISH WITH STIR-FRIED SPINACH

serves 4   *under 20 minutes*

2 tablespoons reduced-sodium soy sauce

2 tablespoons minced scallion

2 tablespoons chopped fresh cilantro

2 garlic cloves, minced

1 tablespoon minced peeled fresh ginger

3 teaspoons Asian (dark) sesame oil

4 (6-ounce) cod, halibut, or flounder fillets

1 pound baby spinach or regular fresh spinach, trimmed

1 Stir together soy sauce, scallion, cilantro, garlic, and ginger in small bowl. Set aside.

2 Heat 1½ teaspoons sesame oil in large nonstick skillet over medium heat. Add fish and cook until fillets begin to brown, about 3 minutes. Carefully turn fish with large spatula. Drizzle fish with soy-sauce mixture and cook just until opaque in center, about 3 minutes. (If sauce starts to stick to bottom of pan before fish is cooked, add a couple of tablespoons water.)

3 Meanwhile, heat remaining 1½ teaspoons oil in another large skillet and set over medium-high heat. Add spinach and cook, stirring constantly, just until spinach is wilted, about 3 minutes.

4 Divide spinach evenly among 4 plates and top each with 1 fish fillet.

 Per serving (1 fillet and ¾ cup spinach): 182 Cal, 5 g Total Fat, 1 g Sat Fat, 852 mg Sod, 5 g Total Carb, 1 g Sugar, 3 g Fib, 30 g Prot.

FISH TACOS WITH MANGO SALSA

serves 4 　gluten free 　under 20 minutes

4 (6-ounce) mahi mahi fillets

½ teaspoon salt

⅓ cup lime juice

2 tablespoons minced scallion

1½ tablespoons minced peeled fresh ginger

1½ teaspoons dark brown sugar

8 (6-inch) corn tortillas, warmed

2 cups shredded leaf lettuce

¼ cup chopped fresh cilantro

½ cup jarred mango or peach salsa

Lime wedges

1 Preheat oven to 450°F. Spray large baking dish with nonstick spray.

2 Sprinkle fish with salt and arrange in single layer in prepared dish.

3 Stir together lime juice, scallion, ginger, and brown sugar in small bowl and pour over fish. Cover and bake until fish is just opaque in center, about 15 minutes.

4 Transfer fish to cutting board and cut into small pieces. Top each tortilla evenly with fish, lettuce, cilantro, and salsa. Fold each taco in half and serve with lime wedges.

6 SmartPoints value

Per serving (2 tacos): 284 Cal, 3 g Total Fat, 1 g Sat Fat, 598 mg Sod, 31 g Total Carb, 7 g Sugar, 4 g Fib, 34 g Prot.

SHRIMP AND SUMMER SQUASH STIR-FRY

¼ cup orange juice

1 tablespoon dry sherry

1 tablespoon tomato paste

3 teaspoons canola oil

2 garlic cloves, minced

1 pound large peeled and deveined shrimp

2 cups thinly sliced yellow squash

2 teaspoons minced jalapeño pepper, with seeds

¾ teaspoon salt

½ avocado, pitted, peeled, and thinly sliced

2 tablespoons chopped fresh cilantro

1 Whisk together orange juice, sherry, and tomato paste in small bowl until smooth. Set aside.

2 Heat wok or large skillet over high heat until drop of water sizzles in it. Add 1½ teaspoons oil and swirl to coat pan. Add garlic and stir-fry until fragrant, about 10 seconds. Add shrimp to wok and arrange in single layer. Cook without stirring 1 minute; then stir-fry until shrimp are lightly browned, 30 seconds longer.

3 Add remaining 1½ teaspoons oil to wok. Add squash, jalapeño, and salt and stir-fry until squash begins to soften, about 1 minute.

4 Add orange juice mixture to wok and stir-fry until shrimp are just opaque in center and squash is crisp-tender, about 1 minute. Remove wok from heat and stir in avocado and cilantro.

5 SmartPoints value

Per serving (1 cup): 219 Cal, 9 g Total Fat, 2 g Sat Fat, 642 mg Sod, 8 g Total Carb, 3 g Sugar, 2 g Fib, 25 g Prot.

CURRIED SHRIMP WITH NAPA CABBAGE

serves 4   *gluten free*

- ¼ cup light (low-fat) coconut milk
- 2 tablespoons reduced-sodium chicken broth
- 1 tablespoon Asian fish sauce
- 1 tablespoon chili-garlic sauce
- ¾ teaspoon cornstarch
- ½ teaspoon sugar
- 4 teaspoons canola oil
- 1 tablespoon minced peeled fresh ginger
- 1 pound large peeled and deveined shrimp
- 1 tablespoon curry powder
- 8 cups (2-inch pieces) Napa cabbage
- ½ teaspoon salt
- Lime wedges

1 Whisk together coconut milk, broth, fish sauce, chili-garlic sauce, cornstarch, and sugar in small bowl. Set aside.

2 Heat wok or large skillet over high heat until drop of water sizzles in it. Add 2 teaspoons oil and swirl to coat pan. Add ginger and stir-fry until fragrant, about 10 seconds. Add shrimp to wok and arrange in single layer. Cook without stirring 1 minute; then stir-fry until shrimp are lightly browned, 30 seconds longer. Stir in curry powder.

3 Add remaining 2 teaspoons oil to wok. Add cabbage and salt and stir-fry 30 seconds. Stir coconut milk mixture and add to wok. Stir-fry until shrimp are just opaque in center and cabbage is crisp-tender, 1–2 minutes. Serve with lime wedges.

 Per serving (1½ cups): 211 Cal, 8 g Total Fat, 1 g Sat Fat, 958 mg Sod, 9 g Total Carb, 3 g Sugar, 2 g Fib, 26 g Prot.

 *If you want to peel and devein the shrimp yourself, you will need about 1⅓ pounds for this recipe.*

Curried Shrimp with Napa Cabbage

GARLICKY SHRIMP AND BROCCOLI WITH TOASTED BREAD CRUMBS

serves 4 *under 20 minutes*

3 cups small broccoli florets

¼ cup water

3 teaspoons extra-virgin olive oil

⅓ cup panko bread crumbs

½ teaspoon grated lemon zest

¼ teaspoon salt

3 garlic cloves, thinly sliced

1 pound large peeled and deveined shrimp

⅓ cup reduced-sodium chicken broth

⅛ teaspoon red pepper flakes

1 tablespoon lemon juice

1 Combine broccoli and water in medium microwavable bowl. Cover with wax paper and microwave on High until crisp-tender, about 4 minutes. Drain and set aside.

2 Meanwhile, heat 1 teaspoon oil in large nonstick skillet over medium heat. Add panko and cook, stirring often, until lightly toasted, about 3 minutes. Transfer panko to small bowl and stir in lemon zest and ⅛ teaspoon salt. Set aside.

3 Wipe out skillet and add 1 teaspoon oil. Set over medium heat. Add garlic and cook, stirring constantly, until light golden, about 1 minute. Add shrimp and cook, stirring often, until shrimp turn pink, about 2 minutes.

4 Add broth, red pepper flakes, and remaining ⅛ teaspoon salt and cook, stirring often, until shrimp are just opaque in center, about 1 minute.

5 Remove skillet from heat and stir in reserved broccoli, lemon juice, and remaining 1 teaspoon oil. Divide shrimp evenly among 4 plates and sprinkle evenly with reserved panko.

 Per serving (¾ cup): 214 Cal, 6 g Total Fat, 1 g Sat Fat, 427 mg Sod, 12 g Total Carb, 2 g Sugar, 2 g Fib, 26 g Prot.

SCALLOPS WITH TOMATO-CAPER SAUCE

serves 4   *gluten free*   *under 20 minutes* 🕐

3 teaspoons olive oil

1 small onion, diced

2 garlic cloves, minced

1 (14½-ounce) can diced tomatoes

½ teaspoon salt

⅛ teaspoon red pepper flakes

4 tablespoons chopped fresh basil

1 tablespoon drained capers

1 pound sea scallops

⅛ teaspoon black pepper

1 To make sauce, heat 2 teaspoons oil in medium skillet over medium-high heat. Add onion and cook, stirring occasionally, until softened, about 5 minutes. Add garlic and cook, stirring constantly, until fragrant, 30 seconds. Add tomatoes, ¼ teaspoon salt, and red pepper flakes and bring to boil. Reduce heat and simmer until slightly thickened, about 5 minutes. Remove from heat and stir in 3 tablespoons basil and capers.

2 Meanwhile, to make scallops, sprinkle scallops with remaining ¼ teaspoon salt and black pepper. Heat remaining 1 teaspoon oil in large skillet over high heat. Add scallops and cook, turning once, until browned and just opaque in center, about 4 minutes.

3 Spoon sauce evenly onto 4 plates. Top evenly with scallops and sprinkle with remaining 1 tablespoon basil.

 Per serving (about 4 scallops and ½ cup sauce): 135 Cal, 4 g Total Fat, 1 g Sat Fat, 935 mg Sod, 10 g Total Carb, 3 g Sugar, 2 g Fib, 15 g Prot.

*Grilled Scallops with
Nectarine-Cucumber Salad*

GRILLED SCALLOPS WITH NECTARINE-CUCUMBER SALAD

 serves 4 gluten free under 20 minutes

- 2 nectarines, pitted and diced
- 2 Kirby cucumbers, thinly sliced
- 1 scallion, thinly sliced
- 1 tablespoon lemon juice
- 1½ teaspoons fresh thyme
- ¾ teaspoon salt
- 2 pinches black pepper
- 2 teaspoons canola oil
- 1 teaspoon grated lemon zest
- 1 teaspoon brown sugar
- ½ teaspoon ground coriander

Pinch ground allspice

- 1 pound sea scallops

1 To make salad, combine nectarines, cucumbers, scallion, lemon juice, ½ teaspoon thyme, ¼ teaspoon salt, and pinch pepper in large bowl.

2 To make scallops, combine oil, lemon zest, brown sugar, remaining 1 teaspoon thyme, remaining ½ teaspoon salt, remaining pinch pepper, coriander, and allspice in medium bowl. Add scallops and toss to coat.

3 Spray ridged grill pan with olive-oil nonstick spray and set over medium-high heat. Place scallops in pan and cook 2 minutes. Lightly spray scallops with olive-oil nonstick spray and turn. Cook until browned and just opaque in center, about 2 minutes longer. Serve scallops with salad.

Per serving (about 4 scallops and ¾ cup salad): 143 Cal, 3 g Total Fat, 0 g Sat Fat, 877 mg Sod, 15 g Total Carb, 8 g Sugar, 2 g Fib, 15 g Prot.

chapter 5

MANGIA!

PASTA & PIZZA

LEMONY PENNE WITH CHICKEN AND BACON

serves 6

- ½ pound penne
- 1 pound skinless boneless chicken breasts, cut into ½-inch pieces
- ¾ teaspoon salt
- ¼ teaspoon black pepper
- 1 tablespoon olive oil
- 1 large shallot, thinly sliced
- ¼ teaspoon red pepper flakes
- 2 zucchini, quartered lengthwise and cut into ½-inch pieces
- 1 cup grape tomatoes, halved
- 3 slices turkey bacon, cooked crisp and crumbled
- ½ cup loosely packed fresh basil leaves, thinly sliced
- 1 teaspoon grated lemon zest
- 2 tablespoons lemon juice

1 Cook pasta according to package directions. Drain, reserving ¼ cup cooking water.

2 Meanwhile, spray large skillet with olive-oil nonstick spray and set over medium-high heat. Sprinkle chicken with ½ teaspoon salt and black pepper. Add to skillet and cook, stirring occasionally, just until chicken is cooked through, about 3 minutes. Transfer chicken to bowl.

3 Add oil to skillet. Add shallot and red pepper flakes and cook, stirring often, until shallot is golden, about 2 minutes. Add zucchini and remaining ¼ teaspoon salt and cook, stirring occasionally, until zucchini are crisp-tender, about 2 minutes.

4 Add pasta, chicken and any accumulated juices, tomatoes, bacon, basil, and lemon zest and juice to skillet and stir to combine. If needed, stir in reserved pasta cooking water, 1 tablespoon at a time, to moisten.

6 SmartPoints value

Per serving (1⅓ cups): 287 Cal, 6 g Total Fat, 1 g Sat Fat, 463 mg Sod, 34 g Total Carb, 3 g Sugar, 2 g Fib, 23 g Prot.

cook's tip

Grit tends to cling to the skin of zucchini, especially if it's from the farmers' market. Give the squash a gentle go-over with a vegetable brush under cold running water just before cooking to clean it thoroughly.

ITALIAN TURKEY AND PASTA CASSEROLE

serves 8

½ pound mezze penne, rotelle, or other small short pasta

1 teaspoon olive oil

1 pound ground lean turkey

3 garlic cloves, minced

1 (15-ounce) can tomato sauce

2 teaspoons dried Italian seasoning

¾ teaspoon salt

¼ teaspoon freshly ground black pepper

1 cup part-skim ricotta

⅓ cup chopped fresh basil plus additional for garnish

2 tablespoons grated pecorino Romano

8 (½-ounce) bocconcini (small fresh mozzarella balls) or 8 (¾-inch) cubes fresh mozzarella

1 Spray flameproof 1½-quart shallow baking dish with nonstick spray.

2 Cook pasta according to package directions. Drain, reserving ¼ cup cooking water. Transfer to large bowl and keep warm.

3 Meanwhile, preheat broiler.

4 Heat oil in large skillet over medium-high heat. Add turkey and cook, breaking apart with wooden spoon, until browned and cooked through, about 5 minutes. Add garlic and cook, stirring constantly, until fragrant, 30 seconds. Stir in tomato sauce, Italian seasoning, ½ teaspoon salt, and pepper and cook until mixture comes to boil.

5 Add ricotta, ⅓ cup basil, pecorino, reserved pasta cooking water, and remaining ¼ teaspoon salt to pasta and stir to combine. Spoon pasta mixture into prepared baking dish. Top evenly with turkey mixture. Arrange mozzarella on top of casserole.

6 Broil 5 inches from heat until cheese is melted, about 1 minute. Sprinkle with additional basil for garnish.

8 SmartPoints value — **Per serving** (⅛ of casserole): 293 Cal, 11 g Total Fat, 5 g Sat Fat, 624 mg Sod, 26 g Total Carb, 3 g Sugar, 2 g Fib, 22 g Prot.

cook's tip

Serve the casserole with a 0 SmartPoints salad of romaine, endive, and radicchio tossed with balsamic vinegar, salt, and black pepper.

BOW-TIE PASTA WITH SAUSAGE AND ESCAROLE

 serves 6 *under 20 minutes*

- 6 ounces bow-tie pasta (about 3 cups)
- 1 teaspoon olive oil
- ½ pound Italian-style turkey sausage, casings removed
- 1 small onion, chopped
- 8 cups chopped escarole
- ¾ cup reduced-sodium chicken broth
- 4 garlic cloves, thinly sliced
- 1 (14½-ounce) can fire-roasted diced tomatoes
- ¼ teaspoon red pepper flakes
- ¼ cup grated Parmigiano-Reggiano

1 Cook pasta according to package directions. Transfer to serving bowl and keep warm.

2 Meanwhile, heat oil in large skillet over medium-high heat. Add sausage and onion and cook, breaking sausage apart with wooden spoon, until sausage is lightly browned, about 5 minutes.

3 Add escarole, broth, and garlic to skillet and cook, stirring often, until escarole is tender, about 5 minutes. Stir in tomatoes and red pepper flakes and cook until heated through, about 1 minute.

4 Add sausage mixture to pasta and toss to combine. Sprinkle with Parmigiano-Reggiano.

5 SmartPoints value

Per serving (1½ cups pasta mixture and 2 teaspoons cheese): 216 Cal, 5 g Total Fat, 1 g Sat Fat, 446 mg Sod, 29 g Total Carb, 3 g Sugar, 4 g Fib, 14 g Prot.

cook's tip

Fire-roasted tomatoes are cooked over an open fire to add a touch of smokiness. Use them in pasta dishes, such as this, sauces, or soups to add another layer of flavor to the dish.

Bow-Tie Pasta with Sausage and Escarole

*Tagliatelle with Limas,
Tomatoes, and Basil*

TAGLIATELLE WITH LIMAS, TOMATOES, AND BASIL

 serves 4 *vegetarian*

6 ounces tagliatelle or fettuccine

1 cup frozen baby lima beans

1 tablespoon olive oil

3 garlic cloves, minced

⅛ teaspoon red pepper flakes

3 cups grape tomatoes, halved

¾ teaspoon salt

¼ teaspoon black pepper

⅓ cup thinly sliced fresh basil

¼ cup grated Parmesan

1 Cook pasta according to package directions, adding lima beans during last 5 minutes of cooking. Drain, reserving ½ cup cooking water.

2 Meanwhile, heat oil in large skillet over medium heat. Add garlic and red pepper flakes and cook, stirring constantly, until fragrant, 30 seconds. Add tomatoes, salt, and black pepper and cook, stirring often, until tomatoes begin to soften, about 4 minutes.

3 Add pasta mixture to skillet. Stir in enough reserved cooking water to moisten. Cook, tossing gently, until heated through, about 1 minute.

4 Remove from heat and stir in basil. Divide evenly among 4 plates and sprinkle each serving with 1 tablespoon Parmesan.

 Per serving (about 1½ cups): 279 Cal, 6 g Total Fat, 2 g Sat Fat, 597 mg Sod, 45 g Total Carb, 5 g Sugar, 4 g Fib, 11 g Prot.

 *cook's tip*

Use any shape of pasta you have on hand for this dish, and instead of grape tomatoes, you can use two medium chopped tomatoes.

RIGATONI WITH ROASTED SQUASH, KALE, AND PINE NUTS

serves 6 *vegetarian*

10 ounces peeled butternut squash, cut into ½-inch pieces (2 cups)

2 small sprigs fresh rosemary

¾ teaspoon salt

¼ teaspoon black pepper

½ pound whole wheat rigatoni

½ pound lacinato kale, stems removed and leaves thinly sliced (about 6 cups)

⅓ cup grated pecorino Romano

1½ tablespoons pine nuts, toasted

1 Preheat oven to 475°F.

2 Line rimmed baking sheet with nonstick foil. Add squash and rosemary sprigs and sprinkle with ¼ teaspoon salt and pepper. Spray squash with olive-oil nonstick spray and toss to coat. Roast until squash is tender, about 15 minutes.

3 Meanwhile, cook rigatoni according to package directions. Drain, reserving ⅓ cup cooking water.

4 Return pasta to cooking pot. Strip leaves from rosemary sprigs and coarsely chop.

5 Add squash, rosemary, reserved pasta cooking water, kale, pecorino, pine nuts, and remaining ½ teaspoon salt to pasta. Toss until kale wilts.

 Per serving (1⅓ cups): 200 Cal, 3 g Total Fat, 1 g Sat Fat, 401 mg Sod, 38 g Total Carb, 1 g Sugar, 7 g Fib, 8 g Prot.

 *cook's tip*

To toast the pine nuts in the microwave, place them in a small microwavable bowl and microwave on High until lightly browned, 45 seconds, stirring once halfway through.

Rigatoni with Roasted Squash, Kale, and Pine Nuts

*Ravioli Salad with
Balsamic Vinaigrette*

RAVIOLI SALAD WITH BALSAMIC VINAIGRETTE

 serves 4 *vegetarian*

¼ cup seasoned dried bread crumbs

1½ tablespoons grated pecorino Romano

⅓ cup low-fat buttermilk

12 large frozen light cheese ravioli

1 tablespoon olive oil

1 tablespoon white balsamic vinegar

1 small garlic clove, crushed through garlic press

¼ teaspoon salt

¼ teaspoon black pepper

1 (5-ounce) bag baby arugula

1 cup grape tomatoes, halved

1 orange bell pepper, thinly sliced

1 Preheat oven to 425°F. Line rimmed baking sheet with nonstick foil.

2 Combine bread crumbs and pecorino in shallow bowl. Put buttermilk in another shallow bowl. Working with 2 ravioli at a time, dip in buttermilk, then crumb mixture, pressing gently to coat. Arrange ravioli on prepared baking sheet in single layer. Lightly spray ravioli with olive-oil nonstick spray. Bake until golden and crisp, about 13 minutes. Let stand 5 minutes to cool before serving.

3 Meanwhile, to make dressing, whisk together oil, vinegar, garlic, salt, and black pepper in large bowl. When ravioli are done, add arugula, tomatoes, and bell pepper to dressing and toss to coat.

4 Divide salad evenly among 4 plates; top each with 3 ravioli.

7 SmartPoints value

Per serving (generous 1 cup salad and 3 ravioli): 245 Cal, 7 g Total Fat, 2 g Sat Fat, 545 mg Sod, 35 g Total Carb, 8 g Sugar, 4 g Fib, 11 g Prot.

GNOCCHI WITH ASPARAGUS, PEAS, AND TOMATOES

serves 4 *vegetarian*

1 (16-ounce) package refrigerated or shelf-stable whole wheat gnocchi

1 pound asparagus, trimmed and cut into 1-inch pieces

1 tablespoon olive oil

½ sweet onion, chopped

4 garlic cloves, minced

4 tomatoes, chopped

½ teaspoon salt

¼ teaspoon black pepper

1 cup frozen petite green peas, thawed

¼ cup thinly sliced fresh basil

2 tablespoons grated pecorino Romano

1 Cook gnocchi according to package directions. Using slotted spoon, transfer gnocchi to medium bowl and set aside. Add asparagus to pot and cook until crisp-tender, 3 minutes. Drain, reserving ¼ cup cooking water.

2 Meanwhile, heat oil in large skillet over medium-high heat. Add onion and garlic. Cook, stirring often, until onion is golden, 2–3 minutes. Add tomatoes, salt, and pepper. Cook, stirring often, until tomatoes are heated through, about 2 minutes.

3 Add gnocchi, asparagus, and peas to skillet. Cook, stirring constantly and adding reserved cooking water as needed to moisten, until heated through, about 3 minutes. Remove from heat. Stir in basil. Divide evenly among 4 bowls and sprinkle evenly with pecorino.

7 SmartPoints value

Per serving (1½ cups pasta and ½ tablespoon cheese): 290 Cal, 5 g Total Fat, 1 g Sat Fat, 811 mg Sod, 52 g Total Carb, 8 g Sugar, 6 g Fib, 11 g Prot.

cook's tip

Use any variety of sweet onion for this recipe. Try Vidalias from Georgia, 1015s (named for the date they are planted, October 15) from Texas, or Oso Sweets from South America.

Gnocchi with Asparagus, Peas, and Tomatoes

PASTA WITH CREAMY SPINACH PESTO

serves 4   *vegetarian*   *under 20 minutes*

½ pound whole wheat spaghetti or linguine

3 tablespoons light cream cheese (Neufchâtel), softened

1 teaspoon lemon juice

4½ cups baby spinach

2 tablespoons water

1½ teaspoons extra-virgin olive oil

2 garlic cloves

½ teaspoon salt

⅛ teaspoon black pepper

4 tablespoons grated Parmesan

1 Cook pasta according to package directions. Drain, reserving ¼ cup cooking water. Transfer pasta to large serving bowl. Add cream cheese and lemon juice and toss until cheese is melted. Keep warm.

2 Meanwhile, to make pesto, puree spinach, water, oil, garlic, salt, and pepper in food processor.

3 Add pesto to pasta mixture and toss to combine. If needed, stir in reserved pasta cooking water, 1 tablespoon at a time, to moisten.

4 Divide pasta evenly among 4 bowls and sprinkle evenly with Parmesan.

8 SmartPoints value

Per serving (1¼ cups): 273 Cal, 6 g Total Fat, 2 g Sat Fat, 472 mg Sod, 46 g Total Carb, 1 g Sugar, 6 g Fib, 13 g Prot.

cook's tip

Add 2 cups of halved cherry tomatoes or 12 ounces chopped cooked skinless chicken breast (adds 2 SmartPoints value per serving) to this simple pasta dish.

w/ grits n cheese instead of Pasta

PASTA WITH RATATOUILLE

serves 6 *vegetarian*

2 teaspoons olive oil

1 onion, chopped

1 small red bell pepper, chopped

4 garlic cloves, minced

1 eggplant, diced

1 small zucchini, diced

2 (14½-ounce) cans diced tomatoes

2 tablespoons drained capers

1 teaspoon dried Italian seasoning

½ teaspoon salt

¼ teaspoon red pepper flakes

½ cup chopped fresh basil

1 (9-ounce) package refrigerated linguine

6 tablespoons freshly grated Parmesan

1 Heat oil in large skillet over medium-high heat. Add onion and bell pepper and cook, stirring often, until vegetables begin to soften, about 3 minutes. Add garlic and cook, stirring constantly, until fragrant, 30 seconds.

2 Add eggplant, zucchini, tomatoes, capers, Italian seasoning, salt, and red pepper flakes. Cook, stirring occasionally, until vegetables are tender, about 5 minutes. Remove from heat and stir in basil.

3 Meanwhile, cook linguine according to package directions and return to pot.

4 Add vegetable mixture to linguine and toss to combine. Divide evenly among 6 plates and sprinkle evenly with Parmesan.

 6 SmartPoints value

Per serving (¾ cup pasta, 1½ cups vegetables, and 1 tablespoon cheese): 260 Cal, 4 g Total Fat, 1 g Sat Fat, 569 mg Sod, 46 g Total Carb, 8 g Sugar, 5 g Fib, 11 g Prot.

 **cook's tip**

Refrigerated pasta is a great time-saver to have on hand. It keeps for several weeks in the refrigerator and cooks in about 5 minutes.

GRILLED SAUSAGE AND PEPPER TORTILLA PIZZAS

- 6 ounces fully cooked chicken sausage (about 2 links), halved lengthwise and thinly sliced
- 1 small red onion, thinly sliced
- 1 small yellow bell pepper, thinly sliced
- 4 (8-inch) whole wheat tortillas
- ½ cup pizza sauce or tomato sauce
- 1 teaspoon dried oregano
- ¾ cup shredded part-skim mozzarella

1 Spray grill rack with nonstick spray and preheat grill to medium or prepare medium fire.

2 Place sausage, onion, and bell pepper in grill basket. Place basket on grill rack and grill, turning basket occasionally, until sausage is browned and vegetables are crisp-tender, about 6 minutes.

3 Spread one side of each tortilla with 2 tablespoons pizza sauce. Top evenly with sausage, onion, and bell pepper. Sprinkle evenly with oregano. Top each pizza with 3 tablespoons mozzarella. Place pizzas on large baking sheet.

4 Using wide spatula, slide pizzas from baking sheet onto grill rack. Cover and grill until edges begin to brown and cheese melts, about 6 minutes. Use wide spatula to remove pizzas from grill.

 Per serving (1 pizza): 213 Cal, 7 g Total Fat, 3 g Sat Fat, 646 mg Sod, 27 g Total Carb, 3 g Sugar, 3 g Fib, 16 g Prot.

 *Depending on your mood, you can make these pizzas with almost any variety of chicken sausage. Try spinach and feta, basil and roasted garlic, Italian-style, or Cajun andouille.*

SPINACH, TOMATO, AND FETA PITA PIZZAS

serves 4　*vegetarian*

- 1 cup part-skim ricotta
- 1 garlic clove, finely minced
- 4 (7-inch) whole wheat pitas
- 1 (10-ounce) package frozen leaf spinach, thawed and squeezed dry
- 1 large tomato, thinly sliced
- ½ cup crumbled feta
- 1 teaspoon dried oregano
- ¼ teaspoon red pepper flakes

1 Preheat oven to 400°F.

2 Stir together ricotta and garlic in small bowl. Spread evenly on pitas to within ½ inch of edges. Top evenly with spinach and tomato and sprinkle with feta and oregano.

3 Arrange pitas in single layer on large baking sheet. Bake until edges of pitas are golden, about 12 minutes. Sprinkle pizzas with red pepper flakes.

 Per serving (1 pizza): 235 Cal, 10 g Total Fat, 6 g Sat Fat, 489 mg Sod, 24 g Total Carb, 3 g Sugar, 5 g Fib, 15 g Prot.

 *cook's tip*

To thaw spinach in the microwave, remove it from the package and place in a microwavable bowl. Microwave on the defrost setting until thawed, about 4 minutes. Place in a sieve and use your hands to squeeze out the liquid.

Spicy White Bean, Caponata, and Arugula Pizzas

SPICY WHITE BEAN, CAPONATA, AND ARUGULA PIZZAS

serves 4   *vegetarian* *under 20 minutes*

1 (7.05-ounce) package mini naan breads

⅔ cup canned cannellini (white kidney) beans, rinsed and drained

1 tablespoon vinegar from cherry peppers

1⅓ cups baby arugula

1 (7-ounce) can caponata, chopped if chunky

⅔ cup shredded reduced-fat Italian four-cheese blend

2 tablespoons sliced hot cherry peppers in vinegar, chopped

1 Preheat broiler.

2 Place naan on baking sheet. Broil 5 inches from heat until lightly browned, 30–60 seconds on each side. Maintain broiler temperature.

3 Combine beans and vinegar in medium bowl and mash with potato masher or fork.

4 Spread bean mixture evenly on naan. Top evenly with arugula, caponata, cheese, and cherry peppers.

5 Broil 5 inches from heat until cheese is melted, about 1 minute.

 Per serving (1 pizza): 255 Cal, 9 g Total Fat, 3 g Sat Fat, 395 mg Sod, 33 g Total Carb, 2 g Sugar, 4 g Fib, 12 g Prot.

cook's tip

If mini naan are not available, you can use four pitas for this recipe.

PIZZA MARGHERITA

serves 4 *vegetarian* *under 20 minutes*

1 artisan thin pizza crust (from 10.2-ounce package)

2 plum tomatoes, thinly sliced

1 garlic clove, minced

1 cup shredded part-skim mozzarella

2 tablespoons thinly sliced fresh basil leaves

½ teaspoon dried oregano

1 Preheat oven to 375°F. Spray baking sheet with nonstick spray.

2 Place crust on baking sheet and bake 2 minutes.

3 Remove from oven and arrange tomatoes on crust and sprinkle with garlic. Top evenly with mozzarella, basil, and oregano. Bake until cheese is melted, about 4 minutes. Cut into 4 wedges.

 Per serving (¼ of pizza): 118 Cal, 5 g Total Fat, 3 g Sat Fat, 238 mg Sod, 10 g Total Carb, 2 g Sugar, 1 g Fib, 9 g Prot.

cook's tip

Fresh basil adds a bang of flavor to this recipe, but in a pinch, you can use a teaspoon of dried basil instead.

Pizza Margherita

SPICY MUSHROOM AND SUN-DRIED TOMATO PIZZA

serves 6 *vegetarian*

- 1 (10-ounce) prebaked thin whole wheat pizza crust
- 2 teaspoons olive oil
- 4 garlic cloves, chopped
- 1 (8-ounce) package sliced cremini mushrooms
- ¼ teaspoon red pepper flakes
- ¼ teaspoon salt
- 1 cup pizza sauce or tomato sauce
- 3 oil-packed sun-dried tomatoes, drained, patted dry with paper towels, and chopped
- ½ cup crumbled goat cheese

1 Preheat oven to 450°F. Spray large baking sheet with nonstick spray.

2 Place crust on baking sheet and bake 5 minutes. Maintain oven temperature.

3 Meanwhile, heat oil in large skillet over medium-high heat. Add garlic and cook, stirring constantly, just until fragrant, about 30 seconds. Add mushrooms, red pepper flakes, and salt and cook, stirring often, until mushrooms are tender, about 3 minutes. Remove from heat.

4 Stir together sauce and sun-dried tomatoes in small bowl. Spread over crust to within ½ inch of edge. Spoon mushroom mixture evenly over sauce. Sprinkle with goat cheese and bake until crust is crisp and cheese is softened, about 8 minutes. Cut into 6 wedges.

 Per serving (⅙ of pizza): 227 Cal, 9 g Total Fat, 5 g Sat Fat, 462 mg Sod, 27 g Total Carb, 3 g Sugar, 5 g Fib, 11 g Prot.

 **cook's tip** *If you don't love spicy food, decrease or omit the red pepper flakes in this recipe.*

MEXICAN VEGETABLE TORTILLA PIZZAS

serves 4   **gluten free**   **vegetarian**

8 (6-inch) corn tortillas

1 teaspoon olive oil

1 small onion, diced

1 small yellow bell pepper, diced

1 small zucchini, diced

1 garlic clove, minced

½ teaspoon ground chipotle chile powder

½ teaspoon salt

1 tomato, diced

1 cup shredded reduced-fat Mexican four-cheese blend

¼ cup chopped fresh cilantro

1 Preheat oven to 450°F.

2 Arrange tortillas in single layer on large baking sheet and bake until crisp, about 5 minutes. Maintain oven temperature.

3 Meanwhile, heat oil in large nonstick skillet over medium heat. Add onion and bell pepper and cook, stirring occasionally, until softened and just beginning to brown, about 2 minutes. Add zucchini and cook, stirring occasionally, until zucchini is tender, about 3 minutes. Stir in garlic, chile powder, and salt and cook, stirring constantly, until fragrant, 30 seconds. Stir in tomato; then remove from heat.

4 Sprinkle tortillas evenly with ½ cup cheese. Top evenly with vegetable mixture; then sprinkle with remaining ½ cup cheese.

5 Bake until cheese melts, 8–10 minutes. Sprinkle evenly with cilantro and serve at once.

Per serving (2 pizzas): 227 Cal, 9 g Total Fat, 4 g Sat Fat, 481 mg Sod, 27 g Total Carb, 3 g Sugar, 5 g Fib, 12 g Prot.

*Zucchini and
Tomato Pita Pizzas*

ZUCCHINI AND TOMATO PITA PIZZAS

serves 4   *vegetarian*   *under 20 minutes*

4   (6-inch) whole wheat pitas

1   teaspoon olive oil

1   zucchini, halved lengthwise and thinly sliced

¼   teaspoon salt

¼   teaspoon black pepper

1   large garlic clove, minced

½   teaspoon dried oregano

16   cherry tomatoes, halved

8   pitted Kalamata olives, sliced

¼   cup crumbled feta

¼   cup shredded part-skim mozzarella

1   scallion, thinly sliced

1 Preheat broiler.

2 Place pitas on baking sheet. Broil 5 inches from heat until lightly browned, 30–60 seconds on each side. Maintain broiler temperature.

3 Heat oil in large nonstick skillet over medium heat. Add zucchini, salt, and pepper and cook, stirring frequently, until zucchini is tender, about 2 minutes. Add garlic and oregano and cook, stirring constantly until fragrant, 30 seconds.

4 Arrange zucchini mixture evenly on pitas. Top with cherry tomatoes and olives; then sprinkle with feta and mozzarella.

5 Broil 5 inches from heat until cheeses are melted, about 1 minute. Sprinkle with scallion; then cut each pita into 4 wedges.

 Per serving (1 pizza): 159 Cal, 6 g Total Fat, 3 g Sat Fat, 507 mg Sod, 21 g Total Carb, 4 g Sugar, 4 g Fib, 7 g Prot.

chapter 6

STRAIGHT FROM THE PANTRY:

START WITH A CAN

SOUTHWESTERN CHICKEN SOUP

serves 4 · *gluten free*

2 teaspoons olive oil

1 pound skinless boneless chicken breasts, cut into ½-inch cubes

½ teaspoon salt

¼ teaspoon freshly ground black pepper

1 onion, chopped

1 small green bell pepper, chopped

1 jalapeño pepper, seeded and chopped

2 garlic cloves, minced

1 tablespoon chili powder

2 teaspoons ground cumin

2 (14½-ounce) cans reduced-sodium chicken broth

1 (14½-ounce) can diced tomatoes, drained

1 cup fresh or frozen corn kernels

1 tablespoon lime juice

½ avocado, pitted, peeled, and cut into 8 slices

¼ cup fresh cilantro leaves

1 Heat 1 teaspoon oil in Dutch oven over medium-high heat. Sprinkle chicken with salt and black pepper. Add chicken to pot and cook, stirring often, until lightly browned and cooked through, about 5 minutes. Transfer to plate.

2 Add remaining 1 teaspoon oil to pot. Add onion, bell pepper, and jalapeño and cook, stirring often, until vegetables are softened, about 3 minutes. Add garlic, chili powder, and cumin and cook, stirring constantly, until fragrant, 30 seconds. Stir in broth, tomatoes, and corn. Cover and bring to boil.

3 Reduce heat to low and simmer, covered, until vegetables are tender, about 8 minutes. Stir in chicken and cook just until heated through, about 2 minutes. Remove from heat and stir in lime juice.

4 Ladle soup evenly into 4 bowls. Top each with 2 slices avocado and sprinkle evenly with cilantro.

 6 SmartPoints value

Per serving (1¾ cups soup with 2 slices avocado): 287 Cal, 10 g Total Fat, 2 g Sat Fat, 988 mg Sod, 22 g Total Carb, 7 g Sugar, 6 g Fib, 28 g Prot.

double duty

Make a double batch of the soup and cover and refrigerate up to 4 days or freeze up to 3 months.

Southwestern
Chicken Soup

QUICK CHICKEN AND CHICKPEA TAGINE

2 teaspoons olive oil

1 pound skinless boneless chicken breasts, cut into 1-inch pieces

½ teaspoon salt

¼ teaspoon black pepper

1 onion, chopped

2 garlic cloves, minced

1 teaspoon paprika

1 teaspoon ground cumin

½ teaspoon ground turmeric

½ teaspoon ground ginger

⅛ teaspoon cinnamon

½ cup reduced-sodium chicken broth

1 (15½-ounce) can chickpeas, rinsed and drained

1 (14½-ounce) can stewed tomatoes

5 pitted prunes, chopped

¼ cup chopped fresh cilantro

1 Heat 1 teaspoon oil in large skillet over medium-high heat. Sprinkle chicken with ¼ teaspoon salt and pepper. Add chicken to skillet and cook, stirring often, until lightly browned and cooked through, about 5 minutes. Transfer to plate.

2 Add remaining 1 teaspoon oil to skillet. Add onion and cook, stirring occasionally, until onion begins to soften, about 3 minutes. Add garlic, paprika, cumin, turmeric, ginger, cinnamon, and remaining ¼ teaspoon salt and cook, stirring constantly, until fragrant, 30 seconds.

3 Stir in broth, chickpeas, tomatoes, and prunes. Cover and bring to boil. Reduce heat to low and simmer, covered, stirring occasionally, 10 minutes. Stir in chicken and cook just until heated through, about 2 minutes.

4 Ladle tagine evenly into 4 bowls, sprinkle with cilantro, and serve at once.

6 SmartPoints value

Per serving (1¼ cups): 324 Cal, 8 g Total Fat, 1 g Sat Fat, 915 mg Sod, 32 g Total Carb, 9 g Sugar, 7 g Fib, 33 g Prot.

cook's tip

Serve the tagine over quinoa (½ cup of cooked quinoa will increase the SmartPoints value by 3).

EXPRESS RED BEANS AND RICE

serves 6 gluten free

- 2 slices turkey bacon, cut crosswise into ½-inch pieces
- 2 teaspoons canola oil
- 1 onion, chopped
- 2 stalks celery, halved lengthwise and sliced
- 2 small assorted-color bell peppers, diced
- 2 garlic cloves, finely chopped
- 1 tablespoon salt-free Cajun seasoning
- 1 teaspoon chopped fresh thyme
- ½ teaspoon salt
- 2 (15½-ounce) cans red kidney beans, rinsed and drained
- 1 (14½-ounce) can diced tomatoes
- ½ cup reduced-sodium chicken broth
- 3 cups instant brown rice

1 Place bacon in large nonstick skillet and cook over medium heat, stirring occasionally, until browned, about 2 minutes. Transfer bacon to paper towel–lined plate.

2 Add oil to skillet. Add onion, celery, and bell peppers. Cook, covered, stirring occasionally, until vegetables are lightly browned and tender, 8–10 minutes. Add garlic, Cajun seasoning, thyme, and salt and cook, stirring constantly, until fragrant, 30 seconds. Stir in beans, tomatoes, and broth and bring to boil. Cook, uncovered, stirring occasionally, until slightly thickened, about 5 minutes.

3 Meanwhile, cook rice according to package directions.

4 Stir bacon into bean mixture and serve over rice.

 Per serving (⅔ cup rice and generous ¾ cup bean mixture): 349 Cal, 5 g Total Fat, 1 g Sat Fat, 826 mg Sod, 65 g Total Carb, 6 g Sugar, 10 g Fib, 13 g Prot.

cook's tip

Serve the beans and rice with a side of slaw. Toss together 6 cups shredded cabbage, ½ cup shredded carrot, 1 thinly sliced scallion, ¼ cup chopped fresh parsley, a splash of cider vinegar, salt, and freshly ground black pepper.

TUSCAN SAUSAGE AND BEAN STEW

serves 4 *under 20 minutes*

2 teaspoons olive oil

6 ounces fully cooked hot Italian-style chicken sausages, halved lengthwise and sliced

1 (10-ounce) package sliced mushrooms

1 small onion, chopped

2 garlic cloves, minced

2 (14½-ounce) cans diced tomatoes

1 (15½-ounce) can cannellini (white kidney) beans, rinsed and drained

1 medium zucchini, halved lengthwise and sliced

2 teaspoons chopped fresh rosemary

¼ teaspoon salt

2 cups baby arugula

¼ cup grated Parmesan

1 Heat oil in Dutch oven over medium-high heat. Add sausages and cook, stirring often, until lightly browned, about 3 minutes. Transfer to plate with slotted spoon.

2 Add mushrooms and onion to pot and cook, stirring often, until vegetables are softened, about 3 minutes. Add garlic and cook, stirring constantly, until fragrant, 30 seconds.

3 Stir in reserved sausages, tomatoes, beans, zucchini, rosemary, and salt and bring to boil. Reduce heat and simmer, uncovered, until vegetables are tender, about 2 minutes. Remove from heat and stir in arugula until wilted.

4 Ladle stew into 4 bowls and top evenly with Parmesan.

6 SmartPoints value

Per serving (1½ cups stew and 1 tablespoon cheese): 296 Cal, 8 g Total Fat, 2 g Sat Fat, 825 mg Sod, 38 g Total Carb, 9 g Sugar, 9 g Fib, 22 g Prot.

cook's tip

For a quick salad to serve with the stew, toss a package of baby spinach with sliced mushrooms, halved cherry tomatoes, lemon juice, salt, and freshly ground black pepper.

Tuscan Sausage and Bean Stew

White Beans with Spinach, Ham, and Goat Cheese

WHITE BEANS WITH SPINACH, HAM, AND GOAT CHEESE

serves 6   *gluten free*

2   teaspoons olive oil

1   (4-ounce) piece thickly sliced lean baked ham, diced

1   onion, chopped

1   small fennel bulb, cored and diced

1   large red or orange bell pepper, diced

2   garlic cloves, minced

1   (15½-ounce) can small white beans, rinsed and drained

2   tablespoons red-wine vinegar

1   tablespoon chopped fresh fennel fronds

¼   teaspoon salt

¼   teaspoon black pepper

1   (6-ounce) bag baby spinach

6   tablespoons crumbled low-fat soft goat cheese

1 Heat 1 teaspoon oil in large nonstick skillet over medium heat. Add ham and cook, stirring occasionally, until lightly browned, 1–2 minutes. Transfer ham to plate.

2 Add remaining 1 teaspoon oil to skillet. Add onion, fennel, and bell pepper. Cook, covered, stirring occasionally, until vegetables are golden, about 5 minutes. Add garlic and cook, stirring constantly, until fragrant, about 30 seconds. Add beans and cook, stirring occasionally, until heated through, about 2 minutes.

3 Remove skillet from heat and stir in vinegar, fennel fronds, salt, and black pepper.

4 Divide spinach evenly among 6 plates. Top evenly with bean mixture, goat cheese, and ham.

 Per serving (1 cup spinach, about ¾ cup bean mixture, 1 tablespoon cheese, and about 2 tablespoons ham) 183 Cal, 5 g Total Fat, 1 g Sat Fat, 391 mg Sod, 23 g Total Carb, 2 g Sugar, 6 g Fib, 12 g Prot.

 *If you can't find a fennel bulb with fronds, substitute chopped fresh dill or parsley.*

CHORIZO AND BLACK-EYED PEA SOUP

serves 4 *gluten free* *under 20 minutes*

2 links fresh chorizo sausage (about 5 ounces), casings removed

1 onion, chopped

1 small green bell pepper, chopped

2 garlic cloves, minced

1 teaspoon no-salt Cajun seasoning

½ teaspoon dried thyme

1 (14½-ounce) can reduced-sodium chicken broth

1 (15½-ounce) can black-eyed peas, rinsed and drained

1 (14½-ounce) can diced tomatoes, undrained

2 cups chopped kale or Swiss chard

1 Cook sausage in Dutch oven over medium-high heat, breaking apart with wooden spoon, until browned, about 3 minutes. Add onion, bell pepper, garlic, Cajun seasoning, and thyme. Cook, stirring often, until vegetables are softened, about 5 minutes.

2 Stir in broth, black-eyed peas, and tomatoes and bring to boil. Reduce heat and simmer, covered, until vegetables are tender, about 5 minutes. Stir in kale and cook until tender, about 3 minutes.

8 SmartPoints value

Per serving (1¾ cups): 310 Cal, 15 g Total Fat, 5 g Sat Fat, 1,000 mg Sod, 28 g Total Carb, 6 g Sugar, 7 g Fib, 18 g Prot.

CURRIED HALIBUT AND VEGETABLE STEW

serves 4 *gluten free*

- 2 teaspoons canola oil
- 2 shallots, thinly sliced
- 2 small zucchini, cut into 2-inch chunks
- 1 red bell pepper, cut into 2-inch chunks
- 2 cups (2-inch pieces) Napa cabbage
- 1 cup light (low-fat) coconut milk
- ½ cup chicken broth
- 2 tablespoons Thai green curry paste
- 2 teaspoons Asian fish sauce
- ¾ pound skinless halibut fillets, cut into 2-inch chunks
- 1 tablespoon thinly sliced fresh basil

Lime wedges

1 Heat oil in large deep, heavy skillet or wok over high heat. Add shallots and stir-fry until softened, about 30 seconds. Add zucchini and bell pepper and stir-fry until crisp-tender, about 2 minutes.

2 Stir in cabbage. Add coconut milk, broth, curry paste, and fish sauce and bring just to boil. Add halibut. Reduce heat and simmer, covered, until halibut is just opaque in center, about 2 minutes. Remove from heat and stir in basil. Serve with lime wedges.

4 SmartPoints value

Per serving (1½ cups): 200 Cal, 9 g Total Fat, 3 g Sat Fat, 708 mg Sod, 12 g Total Carb, 4 g Sugar, 2 g Fib, 18 g Prot.

cook's tip

Brown rice makes a perfect accompaniment to the stew (⅓ cup cooked brown rice will increase the per-serving SmartPoints value by 2).

PORK CHOPS WITH WHITE BEANS AND RADICCHIO

 serves 4 gluten free under 20 minutes

2 garlic cloves, minced

2 teaspoons chopped fresh rosemary

¾ teaspoon salt

½ teaspoon freshly ground black pepper

4 (5-ounce) lean boneless center-cut pork chops, trimmed

2 teaspoons olive oil

2 tablespoons balsamic vinegar

2 (15½-ounce) cans cannellini (white kidney) beans, rinsed and drained

1 small head radicchio, sliced

1 Stir together 1 garlic clove, rosemary, ½ teaspoon salt, and ¼ teaspoon pepper in small bowl. Rub all over pork chops.

2 Heat 1 teaspoon oil in large nonstick skillet over medium heat. Add pork chops and cook, turning once, until instant-read thermometer inserted into sides of chops registers 145°F, about 8 minutes. Transfer to plate and keep warm.

3 Heat remaining 1 teaspoon oil in same skillet. Add remaining 1 garlic clove and cook, stirring constantly until fragrant, about 30 seconds. Add vinegar; then stir in beans. Cook, covered, until beans are heated through, about 3 minutes. Remove skillet from heat. Add radicchio, remaining ¼ teaspoon salt, and remaining ¼ teaspoon pepper and stir just until radicchio is slightly wilted. Stir any accumulated juices from pork chops into beans.

4 Spoon bean mixture evenly onto 4 plates. Top each with a pork chop and serve at once.

 11 SmartPoints value

Per serving (1 pork chop and generous 1 cup bean mixture): 485 Cal, 11 g Total Fat, 3 g Sat Fat, 536 mg Sod, 50 g Total Carb, 2 g Sugar, 11 g Fib, 45 g Prot.

*Pork Chops with White Beans
and Radicchio*

CIOPPINO

serves 6   *gluten free*

2 teaspoons olive oil

1 onion, chopped

1 fennel bulb, cored and chopped

1 red bell pepper, chopped

4 garlic cloves, minced

¼ teaspoon red pepper flakes

½ cup dry white wine

1 (14½-ounce) can chicken broth

1 (28-ounce) can crushed tomatoes

1 (8-ounce) bottle clam juice

1½ teaspoons dried Italian seasoning

½ teaspoon salt

1½ pounds cod, snapper, or other firm white fish, cut into 1-inch pieces

¼ cup chopped fresh parsley

1 Heat oil in Dutch oven over medium-high heat. Add onion, fennel, bell pepper, garlic, and red pepper flakes. Cook, covered, stirring occasionally, until vegetables are softened, about 3 minutes.

2 Add wine and cook, stirring occasionally, until most of liquid evaporates, about 2 minutes. Stir in broth, tomatoes, clam juice, Italian seasoning, and salt. Cover and bring to boil. Reduce heat to low and simmer, covered, until vegetables are tender, about 8 minutes.

3 Stir in fish and cook, covered, until fish is just opaque, about 3 minutes.

4 Ladle soup evenly into 6 bowls, sprinkle with parsley, and serve at once.

 Per serving (1⅔ cups): 183 Cal, 3 g Total Fat, 0 g Sat Fat, 767 mg Sod, 12 g Total Carb, 5 g Sugar, 3 g Fib, 24 g Prot.

TUNA, WHITE BEAN, AND PASTA SALAD

serves 4 • **under 20 minutes**

¼ pound whole wheat fusilli or penne

⅓ cup reduced-sodium chicken broth

¼ cup red-wine vinegar

1½ tablespoons extra-virgin olive oil

1 tablespoon grated lemon zest

½ teaspoon salt

½ teaspoon freshly ground black pepper

1 (15½-ounce) can cannellini (white kidney) beans, rinsed and drained

1 (12-ounce) can water-packed albacore tuna, drained and flaked

1 (7-ounce) jar roasted red peppers (not oil-packed), drained and cut into 1-inch pieces

½ cup diced red onion

⅓ cup chopped fresh parsley

4 teaspoons drained capers

1 Cook pasta according to package directions. Drain and rinse under cold running water and drain again.

2 Meanwhile, whisk together broth, vinegar, oil, lemon zest, salt, and black pepper in large bowl. Add pasta, beans, tuna, roasted peppers, onion, parsley, and capers and toss to combine.

 Per serving (about 1½ cups): 365 Cal, 7 g Total Fat, 1 g Sat Fat, 715 mg Sod, 51 g Total Carb, 3 g Sugar, 9 g Fib, 29 g Prot.

 **cook's tip**

A quarter pound of fusilli is about 1⅔ cups uncooked.

*Salmon Cakes with
Dijon-Herb Sauce*

SALMON CAKES WITH DIJON-HERB SAUCE

serves 4

- 3 (6-ounce) cans skinless boneless wild salmon, drained
- 3 tablespoons reduced-fat mayonnaise
- 3 scallions, chopped
- ½ cup whole wheat panko bread crumbs
- 1 large egg white, lightly beaten
- ¼ teaspoon salt
- ¼ teaspoon black pepper
- 1 teaspoon plus 1 tablespoon olive oil
- 1½ tablespoons lemon juice
- 1 tablespoon Dijon mustard
- 1 tablespoon chopped fresh chives
- 4 cups mixed baby lettuce

1 Place salmon in large bowl and crumble. Add mayonnaise, scallions, ¼ cup panko, egg white, salt, and pepper and stir to combine. With damp hands, shape mixture into 4 patties. Put remaining ¼ cup panko on sheet of wax paper; coat patties with panko.

2 Heat 1 teaspoon oil in large nonstick skillet over medium heat. Add patties and cook, carefully turning once, until crisp and golden, about 8 minutes.

3 Meanwhile, to make sauce, whisk together remaining 1 tablespoon oil, lemon juice, mustard, and chives in small bowl.

4 Divide greens evenly among 4 plates. Top with salmon cakes and drizzle evenly with sauce.

 Per serving (1 salmon cake, 1 cup greens, and 1 tablespoon sauce): 208 Cal, 4 g Total Fat, 1 g Sat Fat, 996 mg Sod, 21 g Total Carb, 15 g Sugar, 3 g Fib, 22 g Prot.

double duty

Make a double batch of the sauce and use it as a dressing for a green salad later in the week.

LINGUINE WITH WHITE BEAN PUTTANESCA

serves 4   *vegetarian*

6 ounces whole wheat linguine

1 tablespoon olive oil

1 onion, chopped

3 garlic cloves, minced

1 teaspoon dried oregano

½ teaspoon red pepper flakes

1 (15½-ounce) can small white beans, rinsed and drained

1 (14½-ounce) can diced tomatoes

12 pimiento-stuffed olives, sliced

2 tablespoons drained capers

¼ teaspoon salt

¼ cup chopped fresh parsley

¼ cup grated pecorino Romano

1 Cook linguine according to package directions, reserving ½ cup cooking water. Place in large serving bowl and keep warm.

2 Meanwhile, heat oil in large skillet over medium-high heat. Add onion and cook, stirring occasionally, until softened, about 5 minutes. Add garlic, oregano, and red pepper flakes and cook, stirring constantly, until fragrant, 30 seconds. Stir in beans, tomatoes, olives, capers, and salt and cook, stirring occasionally, until heated through, about 3 minutes.

3 Add bean mixture and parsley to linguine and toss to combine. Add pasta cooking water, ¼ cup at a time, until mixture is moistened. Sprinkle with pecorino and serve.

10 SmartPoints value

Per serving (1½ cups): 414 Cal, 9 g Total Fat, 2 g Sat Fat, 737 mg Sod, 68 g Total Carb, 4 g Sugar, 17 g Fib, 20 g Prot.

cook's tip

You can use any kind of white beans in this recipe. Try cannellini beans, baby butter beans, great northern, or navy beans.

CURRIED RED LENTIL AND PUMPKIN SOUP

 serves 4 gluten free vegetarian

1 teaspoon canola oil

3 garlic cloves, minced

1 tablespoon grated peeled fresh ginger

4 cups reduced-sodium vegetable broth

1 (15-ounce) can pumpkin (not pie filling)

1 (14-ounce) can light (low-fat) coconut milk

1 cup red lentils, picked over and rinsed

1 tablespoon Thai red curry paste, or more to taste

2 scallions, thinly sliced

1 tablespoon lime juice

4 tablespoons plain reduced-fat Greek yogurt

Chopped fresh cilantro

1 Heat oil in Dutch oven over medium heat. Add garlic and ginger and cook, stirring constantly, until fragrant, 30 seconds.

2 Add broth, pumpkin, coconut milk, lentils, and curry paste. Increase heat to high and bring to boil. Reduce heat and simmer, covered, until lentils are tender, about 20 minutes. Stir in scallions and lime juice.

3 Ladle soup evenly into 4 bowls, top evenly with yogurt, and sprinkle with cilantro.

8 SmartPoints value

Per serving (1¾ cups soup and 1 tablespoon yogurt): 316 Cal, 9 g Total Fat, 4 g Sat Fat, 274 mg Sod, 45 g Total Carb, 8 g Sugar, 18 g Fib, 16 g Prot.

double duty

Make a double batch of the soup and cover and refrigerate up to 4 days or freeze up to 3 months.

CHICKPEA AND ORZO PILAF WITH ZUCCHINI AND MINT

serves 4 *vegetarian* 🍃

1 cup orzo

1 teaspoon olive oil

2 small zucchini, halved lengthwise and sliced

2 garlic cloves, minced

1 teaspoon ground coriander

¾ teaspoon ground cumin

½ teaspoon salt

¼ teaspoon freshly ground black pepper

⅛ teaspoon cinnamon

1 (15½-ounce) can chickpeas, rinsed and drained

1 cup cherry tomatoes, halved

3 tablespoons dried currants

¼ cup chopped fresh mint

½ teaspoon grated lemon zest

1½ tablespoons lemon juice

1 Cook orzo according to package directions. Drain and keep warm.

2 Meanwhile, heat oil in large skillet over medium-high heat. Add zucchini and cook, stirring often, until crisp-tender, about 3 minutes. Add garlic, coriander, cumin, salt, pepper, and cinnamon and cook, stirring constantly, until fragrant, 30 seconds. Add chickpeas, tomatoes, and currants and cook, stirring often, until heated through, about 2 minutes. Stir in orzo.

3 Remove from heat and stir in mint and lemon zest and juice. Serve at once.

 8 SmartPoints value

Per serving (1¼ cups): 306 Cal, 4 g Total Fat, 0 g Sat Fat, 594 mg Sod, 56 g Total Carb, 8 g Sugar, 8 g Fib, 12 g Prot.

cook's tip For even more flavor, sprinkle the pilaf with crumbled reduced-fat feta (2 tablespoons crumbled reduced-fat feta per serving will increase the SmartPoints value by 1).

*Chickpea and Orzo Pilaf
with Zucchini and Mint*

*Bean Burger Salads with Creamy
Cilantro-Lime Dressing*

BEAN BURGER SALADS WITH CREAMY CILANTRO-LIME DRESSING

 serves 4 🍳 *vegetarian* 🍃

BURGERS

- 2 teaspoons olive oil
- 1 shallot, minced
- 1 garlic clove, minced
- 1 (15½-ounce) can pinto beans, rinsed and drained
- ½ cup old-fashioned oats
- 1 large egg white
- 2 tablespoons slivered almonds
- 2 tablespoons chopped fresh cilantro
- 1 teaspoon ground cumin
- ½ teaspoon salt
- ½ teaspoon black pepper

DRESSING

- ¼ cup light sour cream
- ¼ cup lime juice
- 2 tablespoons chopped fresh cilantro
- ¼ teaspoon grated lime zest
- ¼ teaspoon salt

SALAD

- 6 cups torn romaine lettuce
- 4 plum tomatoes, quartered
- ½ English (seedless) cucumber, thinly sliced

1 To make burgers, heat oil in small skillet over medium heat. Add shallot and garlic and cook, stirring often, until softened, 2 minutes. Transfer mixture to food processor.

2 Add beans, oats, egg white, almonds, cilantro, cumin, salt, and pepper to food processor. Pulse until mixture forms chunky puree. Shape mixture into 4 (4-inch) patties.

3 Spray large skillet with nonstick spray and set over medium heat. Add patties and cook, turning once, until well browned, about 6 minutes.

4 Meanwhile, to make dressing, whisk together sour cream, lime juice, cilantro, lime zest, and salt in small bowl.

5 Divide romaine, tomatoes, and cucumber among 4 plates. Top with burgers and drizzle evenly with dressing.

 Per serving (1 salad): 244 Cal, 8 g Total Fat, 2 g Sat Fat, 768 mg Sod, 37 g Total Carb, 7 g Sugar, 10 g Fib, 11 g Prot.

ITALIAN SPINACH AND TORTELLINI SOUP

serves 6 🪐 **vegetarian** 🌿 **under 20 minutes** ⏱

Ingredients

- 2 teaspoons olive oil
- 1 onion, chopped
- 2 zucchini, halved lengthwise and thinly sliced
- 3 garlic cloves, minced
- 1½ teaspoons dried Italian seasoning
- ¾ teaspoon salt
- ⅛ teaspoon red pepper flakes
- ¼ teaspoon freshly ground black pepper
- 3 (14½-ounce) cans reduced-sodium vegetable broth
- 1 (14½-ounce) can diced tomatoes
- ½ cup water
- 1 (9-ounce) package refrigerated mixed cheese tortellini
- 4 cups loosely packed baby spinach or chopped fresh spinach
- ¼ cup chopped fresh basil
- 3 tablespoons freshly grated pecorino Romano

Directions

1 Heat oil in Dutch oven over medium-high heat. Add onion and cook, stirring occasionally, until onion begins to soften, about 3 minutes. Add zucchini and cook, stirring occasionally, until zucchini is crisp-tender, about 3 minutes. Add garlic, Italian seasoning, salt, red pepper flakes, and black pepper and cook, stirring constantly, until fragrant, 30 seconds.

2 Stir in broth, tomatoes, and water. Cover and bring to boil. Stir in tortellini and cook according to timing on package. Stir in spinach and cook until wilted, about 1 minute.

3 Ladle soup evenly into 6 bowls and sprinkle evenly with basil and pecorino.

 5 SmartPoints value

Per serving (about 1¾ cups soup and ½ tablespoon cheese): 199 Cal, 6 g Total Fat, 2 g Sat Fat, 814 mg Sod, 29 g Total Carb, 6 g Sugar, 3 g Fib, 8 g Prot.

cook's tip Serve the soup with a slice of crusty French bread (a 1-ounce piece will increase the per-serving SmartPoints value by 2).

*Italian Spinach and
Tortellini Soup*

chapter 7

NO COOKING REQUIRED:
EASY MEALS

SUMMER COBB SALAD

 serves 6   gluten free   under 20 minutes

3 slices turkey bacon

3 tablespoons olive oil

1 tablespoon water

½ teaspoon grated lemon zest

2 tablespoons lemon juice

1 tablespoon Dijon mustard

½ teaspoon salt

¼ teaspoon black pepper

¼ cup snipped fresh chives

1 (10-ounce) bag chopped romaine hearts

1 (¾-pound) piece skinless boneless roasted turkey or chicken breast, cut into ½-inch pieces

3 small ears corn on the cob, kernels removed

2 cups (½-inch pieces) cantaloupe

½ cup crumbled goat cheese

1 small avocado, halved, pitted, peeled, and diced

1 Microwave bacon according to package directions. Drain on paper towels. Cool and chop.

2 Meanwhile, whisk together oil, water, lemon zest and juice, mustard, salt, and pepper in large bowl. Stir in chives. Add romaine and toss to coat.

3 Place romaine on large platter. Arrange bacon, turkey, corn, cantaloupe, goat cheese, and avocado in rows over romaine. Serve at once.

10 SmartPoints value

Per serving (about 2 cups salad and scant 2 teaspoons dressing): 371 Cal, 21 g Total Fat, 7 g Sat Fat, 485 mg Sod, 22 g Total Carb, 10 g Sugar, 5 g Fib, 26 g Prot.

 *cook's tip*

When shopping for turkey breast, ask for store-roasted turkey instead of the deli variety, which is typically much higher in sodium.

Summer Cobb Salad

QUINOA WITH TURKEY, BRUSSELS SPROUTS, AND CRANBERRIES

serves 4   *gluten free*

1 (1-pound) package frozen cooked quinoa

1 tablespoon olive oil

½ teaspoon grated orange zest

¼ cup orange juice

1 small shallot, minced

1 teaspoon white balsamic vinegar

½ teaspoon salt

¼ teaspoon black pepper

½ pound Brussels sprouts, thinly sliced

1 (6-ounce) slice smoked turkey breast, diced

¼ cup dried cranberries, chopped

8 escarole leaves

¼ cup toasted walnuts, coarsely chopped

1 Microwave quinoa according to package directions. Transfer to sieve set over bowl. Let stand, tossing occasionally with wooden spoon, until well drained and slightly cooled.

2 Meanwhile, whisk together oil, orange zest and juice, shallot, vinegar, salt, and pepper in large bowl. Add quinoa, Brussels sprouts, turkey, and cranberries and toss to coat.

3 Line 4 plates with escarole. Top evenly with quinoa mixture and walnuts.

Per serving (2 escarole leaves, 1¼ cups quinoa mixture, and 1 tablespoon walnuts) 320 Cal, 12 g Total Fat, 2 g Sat Fat, 527 mg Sod, 41 g Total Carb, 9 g Sugar, 6 g Fib, 16 g Prot.

cook's tip

Escarole, a member of the endive family, has broad, slightly curved, pale green leaves and a milder flavor than its curly cousin. If you have any leftover greens, coarsely chop them and add to a soup or stew.

THAI BEEF SALAD

3   tablespoons lime juice

1   tablespoon brown sugar

2   teaspoons Asian fish sauce

½   teaspoon Thai red
    curry paste

¾   pound (½-inch thick) sliced
    lean roast beef, cut into
    thin strips

½   small yellow or orange bell
    pepper, diced

2   plum tomatoes, cut into
    thin wedges

1   small onion, thinly sliced

1   small cucumber, peeled,
    halved lengthwise, and
    thinly sliced

¼   cup chopped fresh cilantro

¼   cup chopped fresh mint

6   large Bibb or leaf
    lettuce leaves

¼   cup unsalted peanuts,
    finely chopped

Lime wedges

1 To make dressing, whisk together lime juice, brown sugar, fish sauce, and curry paste in small bowl.

2 Toss together roast beef, bell pepper, tomatoes, onion, cucumber, cilantro, and mint in large bowl. Add dressing and toss to mix well.

3 Place lettuce on platter and top with roast beef mixture. Sprinkle evenly with peanuts and serve with lime wedges.

 Per serving (⅙ of salad): 172 Cal, 7 g Total Fat, 2 g Sat Fat, 196 mg Sod, 9 g Total Carb, 5 g Sugar, 2 g Fib, 17 g Prot.

ROAST BEEF AND ARUGULA SALAD WITH WHEAT BERRIES

 serves 6 *under 20 minutes*

1½ tablespoons olive oil

1½ tablespoons red-wine vinegar

1½ teaspoons coarse-grained mustard

1½ teaspoons chopped fresh thyme

1 teaspoon chopped fresh rosemary

1 garlic clove, crushed through garlic press

¾ teaspoon salt

¼ teaspoon black pepper

2 cups frozen cooked wheat berries, thawed

2 carrots, thinly sliced

1 small fennel bulb, cored and thinly sliced

½ cup jarred roasted red peppers (not oil-packed), drained and sliced

1 (5-ounce) container baby arugula

¾ pound thickly sliced lean roast beef, cut into 1-inch strips

1 To make dressing, whisk together oil, vinegar, mustard, thyme, rosemary, garlic, salt, and black pepper in small bowl.

2 Place wheat berries, carrots, fennel, and roasted peppers in large bowl. Add 2 tablespoons dressing and toss to coat.

3 Arrange arugula on serving platter and drizzle with remaining dressing. Top with wheat berry mixture and arrange roast beef on top.

 Per serving (1¼ cups arugula, 1 cup wheat berry mixture, and 2 ounces roast beef) 218 Cal, 7 g Total Fat, 2 g Sat Fat, 874 mg Sod, 23 g Total Carb, 3 g Sugar, 5 g Fib, 17 g Prot.

SHRIMP SALAD WITH FENNEL, RED ONION, AND ORANGE

serves 4  *gluten free*

2 tablespoons lemon juice

2 teaspoons extra-virgin olive oil

¼ teaspoon black pepper

3 large navel oranges

1 pound cooked medium peeled and deveined shrimp

1 fennel bulb, cored and very thinly sliced

½ small red onion, thinly sliced

12 pitted Kalamata olives

1 tablespoon chopped fresh fennel fronds or parsley

1 To make dressing, whisk together lemon juice, oil, and pepper in small bowl.

2 To section oranges, cut slice off top and bottom end. Stand orange and slice off peel and white pith, turning orange as you cut. Hold fruit over large bowl to catch juices and cut between membranes to release sections, allowing sections and juice to fall into bowl.

3 Add shrimp, fennel, onion, olives, fennel fronds, and dressing to oranges and toss to combine.

 Per serving (about 2 cups): 257 Cal, 6 g Total Fat, 1 g Sat Fat, 1,191 mg Sod, 25 g Total Carb, 14 g Sugar, 6 g Fib, 28 g Prot.

cook's tip

Cooked and peeled shrimp are pricey, but they're worth it for the prep time you save. Buying them in the frozen food department and thawing them at home is usually a bit less expensive than getting them in the seafood department.

SALMON PANZANELLA WITH FRESH BASIL

1   teaspoon grated lemon zest

2   tablespoons lemon juice

1   tablespoon red-wine vinegar

2   teaspoons olive oil

¼   teaspoon salt

¼   teaspoon black pepper

4   tomatoes, cut into ¾-inch pieces

½   cup roasted red peppers (not oil-packed), drained and coarsely chopped

½   small red onion, thinly sliced

8   Kalamata olives, pitted and halved

1   (14¾-ounce) can wild Alaskan salmon, drained

1   small English (seedless) cucumber, quartered lengthwise and sliced

4   (¾-inch-thick) slices whole wheat ciabatta bread, toasted and cut into cubes

1½   cups fresh basil leaves, torn

1 Whisk together lemon zest and juice, vinegar, oil, salt, and black pepper in large bowl. Stir in tomatoes, roasted peppers, onion, and olives and let stand 10 minutes.

2 Meanwhile, remove skin and bones from salmon and discard. Break salmon into large pieces. Gently stir salmon, cucumber, and bread into tomato mixture. Let stand until bread soaks up some of juices, about 5 minutes. Stir in basil and serve at once.

 Per serving (2 cups): 288 Cal, 10 g Total Fat, 1 g Sat Fat, 855 mg Sod, 26 g Total Carb, 8 g Sugar, 5 g Fib, 26 g Prot.

cook's tip

Toss some more veggies into this salad if you have them on hand. Fresh fennel, carrots, radishes, and celery would all be delicious additions.

*Salmon Panzanella
with Fresh Basil*

Pan Bagnat

PAN BAGNAT

serves 4   *under 20 minutes*

3 tablespoons red-wine vinegar

3 tablespoons chopped fresh parsley

2 tablespoons reduced-sodium chicken broth

1 tablespoon olive oil

1 garlic clove, minced

¼ teaspoon black pepper

1 (8-ounce) loaf Italian bread

4 radishes, thinly sliced

¼ cup pitted Kalamata olives, coarsely chopped

2 (5-ounce) cans water-packed tuna, drained

1 small red onion, thinly sliced

2 tomatoes, thinly sliced

1 To make dressing, whisk together vinegar, parsley, broth, oil, garlic, and pepper in small bowl.

2 Using serrated knife, split bread in half lengthwise, making bottom of loaf slightly thicker than top. Use your fingers to pull out and discard some of soft interior of bread. Brush inside of top half of loaf with half of dressing.

3 Layer bottom section of bread with radishes, then olives. Top with tuna and onion, then tomatoes. Drizzle with remaining dressing. Cover with bread top and cut into 4 sandwiches.

5 SmartPoints value

Per serving (1 sandwich): 236 Cal, 7 g Total Fat, 1 g Sat Fat, 513 mg Sod, 26 g Total Carb, 3 g Sugar, 3 g Fib, 18 g Prot.

cook's tip

Perfect for a picnic or an office lunch, the flavor of these sandwiches actually improves if you wrap them individually and refrigerate a couple of hours.

THAI SHRIMP AND NOODLE SALAD

serves 4 *under 20 minutes*

2 tablespoons lime juice

1½ tablespoons reduced-sodium soy sauce

2 teaspoons chili-garlic sauce

1 teaspoon sugar

1 teaspoon canola oil

1 pound cooked medium peeled and deveined shrimp

2 ounces thin rice stick noodles

½ English (seedless) cucumber, cut into matchstick strips

1 cup coarsely shredded carrots

2 tablespoons chopped fresh mint

1 To make dressing, whisk together lime juice, soy sauce, chili-garlic sauce, sugar, and oil in small bowl.

2 Place shrimp in large bowl. Add 1 tablespoon dressing and toss to coat.

3 Meanwhile, prepare noodles according to package directions. Drain, rinse with cold water, and drain again.

4 Add noodles, cucumber, carrots, mint, and remaining dressing to shrimp and toss to coat.

 4 SmartPoints value

Per serving (about 1½ cups): 225 Cal, 3 g Total Fat, 1 g Sat Fat, 1,355 mg Sod, 20 g Total Carb, 4 g Sugar, 2 g Fib, 27 g Prot.

 *cook's tip*

Rice stick noodles don't actually "cook"—they simply soak in boiling water for less than 5 minutes to soften.

SHRIMP AND SNAP PEA SALAD WITH LIME

2 tablespoons canola oil

1 teaspoon grated lime zest

2 tablespoons lime juice

¾ teaspoon kosher salt

1 pound cooked medium peeled and deveined shrimp

4 scallions, thinly sliced

3 radishes, thinly sliced

2½ cups sugar snap peas, trimmed and halved

2 cups coarsely shredded carrots

2 red bell peppers, thinly sliced

1 large mango, peeled, pitted, and diced

1 serrano or jalapeño pepper, seeded and minced

¼ cup chopped fresh mint

¼ cup chopped fresh cilantro

6 tablespoons dry-roasted salted peanuts, chopped

Whisk together oil, lime zest and juice, and salt in large bowl. Add shrimp, scallions, radishes, peas, carrots, bell peppers, mango, serrano, mint, and cilantro and toss to combine. Sprinkle with peanuts and serve at once.

4 SmartPoints value **Per serving** (1⅔ cups): 279 Cal, 11 g Total Fat, 2 g Sat Fat, 990 mg Sod, 27 g Total Carb, 15 g Sugar, 6 g Fib, 22 g Prot.

cook's tip

Serve this salad on a bed of baby spinach or salad greens, or for an extra 3 SmartPoints, spoon each serving over ½ cup cooked and cooled rice noodles.

SHRIMP SALAD WITH PAPAYA AND MANGO

serves 6   *gluten free*

¼ cup lemon juice

1 tablespoon olive oil

¼ teaspoon salt

¼ teaspoon black pepper

1¼ pounds cooked large peeled and deveined shrimp

1 large Granny Smith apple, cored and cut into thin pieces

1 mango, peeled, pitted, and diced

1 papaya, peeled, halved, seeded, and diced

½ cup thinly sliced red onion

1 jalapeño pepper, seeded and minced

2 tablespoons chopped fresh cilantro

1 To make dressing, whisk together lemon juice, oil, salt, and black pepper in small bowl.

2 Transfer 2 tablespoons dressing to large bowl. Add shrimp and let stand 10 minutes.

3 Add apple, mango, papaya, onion, jalapeño, and cilantro and toss to coat.

2 SmartPoints value

Per serving (1½ cups): 208 Cal, 4 g Total Fat, 1 g Sat Fat, 996 mg Sod, 21 g Total Carb, 15 g Sugar, 3 g Fib, 22 g Prot.

cook's tip

While the shrimp marinate, prep the fruit, onion, and jalapeño for the salad.

Shrimp Salad with Papaya and Mango

White Bean, Roasted Pepper, and Arugula Salad

WHITE BEAN, ROASTED PEPPER, AND ARUGULA SALAD

serves 4 • **gluten free** • **vegetarian** • **under 20 minutes**

2 tablespoons water

1½ tablespoons extra-virgin olive oil

1 tablespoon balsamic vinegar

½ teaspoon salt

¼ teaspoon freshly ground black pepper

1 (15½-ounce) can cannellini (white kidney) beans, rinsed and drained

1 cup grape tomatoes, halved

1 (7-ounce) jar roasted red peppers (not oil-packed), drained and thinly sliced

1 (5-ounce) package baby arugula

1 ounce shaved Parmesan

1 Whisk together water, oil, vinegar, salt, and black pepper in large bowl. Add beans, tomatoes, and roasted peppers and toss to combine. Add arugula and toss to coat.

2 Divide salad evenly among 4 plates and top evenly with Parmesan.

 6 SmartPoints value

Per serving (2 cups): 230 Cal, 8 g Total Fat, 2 g Sat Fat, 523 mg Sod, 31 g Total Carb, 4 g Sugar, 6 g Fib, 12 g Prot.

 **cook's tip**

Pump up the veggies in this salad by adding a chopped cucumber and some thinly sliced red onion.

BLACK BEAN, TOMATO, AND CORN SALAD TOSTADAS

 serves 4 gluten free vegetarian under 20 minutes

- 3 tablespoons lime juice
- 1 teaspoon olive oil
- 1 teaspoon ground cumin
- ¼ teaspoon salt
- 1 cup canned black beans, rinsed and drained
- ½ cup grape tomatoes, halved
- ¼ cup thawed frozen corn kernels
- ¼ cup diced canned green chiles
- 2 tablespoons minced red onion
- 2 tablespoons fresh cilantro leaves
- 1 clove garlic, minced
- 4 (6-inch) corn tortillas, toasted

1 Whisk together lime juice, oil, cumin, and salt. Add beans, tomatoes, corn, chiles, onion, cilantro, and garlic and stir to combine.

2 Place tortillas on 4 plates and top evenly with black bean mixture. Serve at once.

 4 SmartPoints value

Per serving (1 tostada): 140 Cal, 2 g Total Fat, 0 g Sat Fat, 425 mg Sod, 26 g Total Carb, 2 g Sugar, 7 g Fib, 6 g Prot.

 *double duty*

Make a double batch of the salad and serve it at another meal on a bed of salad greens or inside halved pitas.

*Black Bean, Tomato, and
Corn Salad Tostadas*

BLACK BEAN AND AVOCADO SANDWICHES

serves 4 *vegetarian* 🍃 *under 20 minutes* ⏱

1 (15½-ounce) can black beans, rinsed and drained

2 tablespoons lemon juice

1 tablespoon olive oil

1 garlic clove, chopped

1 teaspoon ground cumin

¼ teaspoon salt

½ avocado, halved, pitted, and peeled

8 slices reduced-calorie whole wheat bread, toasted

1 (7-ounce) jar roasted red peppers (not oil-packed), drained and thinly sliced

1 cup baby spinach

½ small English (seedless) cucumber, thinly sliced

1 Puree beans, lemon juice, oil, garlic, cumin, and salt in food processor.

2 Place avocado in small bowl and mash with fork.

3 Spread about ¼ cup bean mixture on each of 4 slices toast. Top evenly with roasted peppers, spinach, and cucumber.

4 Spread avocado evenly on remaining 4 slices toast and cover sandwiches. Cut in half and serve at once.

4 SmartPoints value

Per serving (1 sandwich): 287 Cal, 9 g Total Fat, 1 g Sat Fat, 795 mg Sod, 45 g Total Carb, 5 g Sugar, 14 g Fib, 13 g Prot.

cook's tip

Change up the veggie toppings for these sandwiches depending on what you have on hand. You can use sliced tomatoes, red onion, or radishes, and any type of salad greens can stand in for baby spinach.

LENTIL SALAD WITH FETA AND DILL

serves 4   gluten free   vegetarian   under 20 minutes

2 tablespoons red-wine vinegar

1 tablespoon olive oil

1 tablespoon whole-grain Dijon mustard

¼ teaspoon salt

¼ teaspoon black pepper

1½ cups fully cooked refrigerated lentils

2 carrots, diced

1 shallot, finely chopped

½ small fennel bulb, cored and diced

2 tablespoons chopped fresh dill

½ cup crumbled reduced-fat feta

Whisk together vinegar, oil, mustard, salt, and pepper in large bowl. Stir in lentils, carrots, shallot, fennel, and dill. Divide evenly among 4 plates and top evenly with feta.

3 SmartPoints value

Per serving (1½ cups salad and 2 tablespoons feta): 118 Cal, 5 g Total Fat, 3 g Sat Fat, 238 mg Sod, 10 g Total Carb, 2 g Sugar, 1 g Fib, 9 g Prot.

Brown Rice and Veggie Bowls
with Ginger-Lime Dressing

BROWN RICE AND VEGGIE BOWLS WITH GINGER-LIME DRESSING

serves 4 · gluten free · vegetarian · under 20 minutes

- 2 tablespoons lime juice
- 2 tablespoons fresh cilantro leaves
- 4 teaspoons Asian (dark) sesame oil
- 1 tablespoon water
- 2 teaspoons honey
- 2 teaspoons grated peeled fresh ginger
- ¼ teaspoon salt
- 1½ cups cooked brown rice, at room temperature
- 1 (15½-ounce) can black beans, rinsed and drained
- ½ avocado, pitted, peeled, and diced
- 1 small red onion, finely chopped
- 1 carrot, cut into matchstick strips
- 1 red bell pepper, chopped
- 1 cup grape tomatoes, quartered
- 1 mango, peeled, pitted, and diced
- Fresh cilantro leaves

1 Puree lime juice, cilantro leaves, sesame oil, water, honey, ginger, and salt in blender or mini-food processor.

2 Combine rice, beans, avocado, onion, carrot, bell pepper, tomatoes, and mango in large bowl and toss to combine. Add lime juice mixture and toss to coat.

3 Divide evenly among 4 bowls and sprinkle with cilantro.

8 SmartPoints value

Per serving (1½ cups): 323 Cal, 10 g Total Fat, 1 g Sat Fat, 570 mg Sod, 53 g Total Carb, 13 g Sugar, 13 g Fib, 10 g Prot.

cook's tip

Use a packet of precooked brown rice or brown rice from a Chinese take-out restaurant for this recipe.

*Pork Chops with Fig Sauce and
Parmesan Green Beans, 60*

RECIPES BY SMARTPOINTS VALUE

2 SmartPoints

Cioppino, 162
Grilled Scallops with Nectarine-Cucumber
  Salad, 121
Salmon Cakes with Dijon-Herb Sauce, 165
Scallops with Tomato-Caper Sauce, 119
Shrimp Salad with Papaya and Mango, 188
Soy-Glazed Fish with Stir-Fried Spinach, 113

3 SmartPoints

Asian Turkey Lettuce Wraps, 69
Chicken with Cherry Tomato–Basil Sauce, 7
Chicken with Roasted Red Bell Pepper–Basil
  Sauce, 4
Crispy Jalapeño-Lime Fish Cakes, 109
Flounder with Basil-Mint Tomatoes, 108
Gingery Beef and Mushroom Lettuce Wraps, 82
Grilled Pork with Arugula and Tomato Salad, 54
Grilled Tuna with Fennel, Orange, and
  Olive Salad, 103
Lentil Salad with Feta and Dill, 195
Mozzarella, Roasted Pepper, and
  Basil Omelette, 88
Pizza Margherita, 142
Pork Medallions with Indian-Spiced
  Squash Sauté, 57
Shrimp Salad with Fennel, Red Onion,
  and Orange, 181
Steak with Fresh Tomato and Corn Salsa, 34

4 SmartPoints

Asian Chicken and Veggie Tortilla Wraps, 22
Black Bean and Avocado Sandwiches, 194
Black Bean, Tomato, and Corn Salad
  Tostadas, 192
Broiled Steak and Peppers with Creamy
  Salsa Verde, 45
Catfish and Vegetable Stir-Fry, 110
Chicken and Vegetable Kebabs with
  Creamy Pesto, 13
Chicken Sauté with Bell Peppers and
  Goat Cheese, 16
Creamy Chicken Paprikash with Fresh Dill, 14
Curried Halibut and Vegetable Stew, 159
Garlicky Shrimp and Broccoli with Toasted
  Bread Crumbs, 118

Grilled Flank Steak with Clementine Salad, 46
Grilled Flank Steak with Tomato-Fennel Salad, 48
Grilled Korean Steak in Lettuce Cups, 37
Huevos Mexicanos, 87
Lemon Pork and Snap Pea Stir-Fry, 58
Peppered Tuna with Lemongrass
  Vinaigrette, 104
Pork Chops with Ginger-Lime Peach Salsa, 59
Roast Beef and Arugula Salad with
  Wheat Berries, 180
Rosemary Lamb Chops with Balsamic
  Tomatoes, 65
Salmon with Coconut-Tomato Sauce, 98
Shrimp and Snap Pea Salad with Lime, 187
Spice-Crusted Steak with Wild Mushrooms, 39
Thai Beef and Pea Shoot Salad, 43
Thai Beef Salad, 179
Thai Shrimp and Noodle Salad, 186
White Beans with Spinach, Ham, and
  Goat Cheese, 157
Zucchini and Tomato Pita Pizzas, 147

5 SmartPoints

Bow-Tie Pasta with Sausage and Escarole, 126
Curried Shrimp with Napa Cabbage, 116
Filets Mignons with Orange and
  Avocado Salad, 49
Honey-Mustard Roasted Salmon, 102
Italian Spinach and Tortellini Soup, 172
Moo Shu Pork Stir-Fry, 53
Pan Bagnat, 185
Rigatoni with Roasted Squash, Kale, and
  Pine Nuts, 130
Salmon Panzanella with Fresh Basil, 182
Sautéed Chicken with Lemon-Caper Sauce, 26
Shrimp and Summer Squash Stir-Fry, 115
Sirloin and Arugula Salad with
  Balsamic Vinaigrette, 44
Soba Chicken Noodle Bowl, 20
Spice-Rubbed Mango-Glazed Pork
  Tenderloin, 52

6 SmartPoints

Bean Burger Salads with Creamy Cilantro-Lime
  Dressing, 171
Cannellini Beans with Kale and Bacon, 84

Chicken Thighs with Ginger-Plum Sauce, 25
Eggs with Polenta and Spicy Black Beans, 85
Fish Tacos with Mango Salsa, 114
Grilled Chicken and Corn Salad with
　Yogurt-Lime Dressing, 3
Grilled Chicken Kebabs with Orzo, 11
Grilled Sausage and Pepper Tortilla Pizzas, 138
Lemony Penne with Chicken and Bacon, 124
Mexican Vegetable Tortilla Pizzas, 145
Pasta with Ratatouille, 137
Pork Chops with Braised Cabbage
　and Raisins, 63
Pork Chops with Fig Sauce and Parmesan
　Green Beans, 60
Quick Beef and Pinto Bean Chili, 79
Quick Chicken and Chickpea Tagine, 152
Red Curry Chicken with Cauliflower, 30
Rosemary Chicken with Balsamic-Glazed
　Onions, 2
Sautéed Halibut with Coconut Rice
　and Mango Salsa, 107
Southwestern Chicken Soup, 150
Spiced Beef Ragu, 78
Steak and Pepper Sandwiches with
　Chipotle Mayo, 51
Thai Turkey, Noodle, and Asparagus Salad, 73
Tuscan Chicken Sausage and Bean Stew, 154
White Bean, Roasted Pepper, and
　Arugula Salad, 191

7 SmartPoints

Beef and Portobello Burgers, 81
Chicken and Vegetable Fried Rice, 15
Gnocchi with Asparagus, Peas,
　and Tomatoes, 134
Pasta Soup with Cannellini and Escarole, 91
Pork Chops and Vegetables with Yellow
　Curry Sauce, 62
Ravioli Salad with Balsamic Vinaigrette, 133
Spicy Mushroom and Sun-Dried
　Tomato Pizza, 144
Spinach, Tomato, and Feta Pita Pizzas, 139
Stir-Fried Chicken with Vegetables, 29

8 SmartPoints

Barbecue Ranch Chicken Salad, 8
Brown Rice and Veggie Bowls with Ginger-Lime
　Dressing, 197
Chicken with Pasta and Puttanesca Sauce, 10
Chickpea and Orzo Pilaf with Zucchini
　and Mint, 168
Chorizo and Black-Eyed Pea Soup, 158

Curried Red Lentil and Pumpkin Soup, 167
Falafel Sandwiches with Avocado
　Lime Sauce, 95
Italian Turkey and Pasta Casserole, 125
Mexican Black Bean Soup, 92
Pasta with Creamy Spinach Pesto, 136
Peppered Sirloin with Black Bean and
　Avocado Salad, 36
Salmon with Thai Slaw, 101
Spicy White Bean, Caponata, and
　Arugula Pizzas, 141
Tagliatelle with Limas, Tomatoes, and Basil, 129
Teriyaki Turkey Burgers, 68
Thai Ginger Chicken Burgers, 19
Tuna, White Bean, and Pasta Salad, 163
Turkey and White Bean Chili, 70

9 SmartPoints

Beef and Ziti with Roasted Peppers and
　Green Olives, 75
Chicken Sausages and Vegetables over
　Herbed Polenta, 31
Express Red Beans and Rice, 153
Quinoa with Turkey, Brussels Sprouts,
　and Cranberries, 178
White Bean and Almond Burgers, 93

10 SmartPoints

Braised Chicken with Feta and Olives, 23
Harissa-Spiced Sirloin with Mint Couscous, 40
Linguine with White Bean Puttanesca, 166
Summer Cobb Salad, 176
Turkey Picadillo Tacos, 74
Turkey Taco Salad, 76

11 SmartPoints

Pork Chops with White Beans and Radicchio, 160

INDEX